"It's All Grace"
the best of Eppinga

JACOB D. EPPINGA

FAITH
ALIVE®
Christian Resources

Grand Rapids, Michigan

Cover Illustration: iStockphoto

Unless otherwise indicated, the Scripture quotations in this publication are from the HOLY BIBLE, NEW INTERNATIONAL VERSION, ©1973, 1978, 1984, International Bible Society. Used by permission of Zondervan Bible Publishers.

It's All Grace: The Best of Eppinga © 2008 by Faith Alive Christian Resources, 2850 Kalamazoo Ave. SE, Grand Rapids, MI 49560. 1-800-333-8300.

Printed in the United States of America.
Library of Congress Cataloging-in-Publication Data

Eppinga, Jacob D.
It's all grace : the best of Eppinga / Jacob D. Eppinga.
   p. cm.
   ISBN 978-1-59255-466-9 (alk. paper)
   1. Meditations. I. Title.

 BV4832.3.E67 2008
 242--dc22   2008031367

10 9 8 7 6 5 4

Contents

"The time has come," the Walrus said,
"To talk of many things:
Of shoes—and ships—and sealing wax—
Of cabbages—and kings—
And why the sea is boiling hot—
And whether pigs have wings."

—LEWIS CARROLL.
"THE WALRUS AND THE CARPENTER"

From *Through the Looking-Glass and What Alice Found There,* 1872

Foreword

Y ou might say Rev. Jacob Dirk Eppinga (1917-2008) was pastor to the entire Christian Reformed Church in North America. Although he served LaGrave Avenue CRC, a large congregation in downtown Grand Rapids, Michigan, for 33 of his 63 years in ministry, he is best known for his column "Of Cabbages and Kings," which appeared in the denomination's magazine, *The Banner,* from the fall of 1968 to the fall of 2008.

It is no small feat to write a column for 40 years, let alone remain a magazine's most popular author (a fact borne out by every survey conducted by *The Banner* during that time). Well-read, a keen observer of human life, and a gifted storyteller, Rev. Eppinga stayed true to the magazine's original request to write using "a light pen with a point."

With wit and wisdom he inspired us through stories about everything from blue marbles to shaggy dogs to dreams of heaven—pointing always to the grace and goodness of God shown to us through Jesus Christ.

He also taught us to laugh at ourselves. In an interview on the 30th anniversary of his column, he mused: "All those nights our consistory spent pondering issues like whether we should serve coffee after church. Was it worth it? We have only one life to live. We shouldn't take ourselves too seriously. Sometimes we have to laugh at ourselves, to remember that we're all in this church together."

In featuring "the best of Eppinga," this compilation focuses especially on the last decade of his columns. But you'll also find it somewhat autobiographical. Like any good pastor, Rev. Eppinga could not help but draw stories from his own life—sharing the best of himself (including his foibles) with the church he loved. We've also included a few family favorites chosen by his children, Dick, Jay, Susan, and Deanna and their families.

In giving thanks for the life and stories of Rev. Eppinga, a word of thanks is also in order to the "inimitable Mrs. Ruth Snoek," as Rev. Eppinga called her, who was his administrative assistant at LaGrave for nearly 30 years. She continued to assist him in retirement, readying the final drafts of his "Cabbages"—which he either hand-wrote or pounded out on his failing 1914 Woodstock typewriter.

From his very first article ("Always Something") to his last ("Of Death and Grace"), Rev. Eppinga remained a faithful, creative pastor who encouraged *Banner* readers. Even during his final hours, he imparted one more gift to his family and to us, one more—albeit brief—story pointing to the reality of the kingdom of heaven:

Asked about the look of wonder on his face as death drew near, Rev. Eppinga replied, "I see angels. . . . Lots of them."

Jena (Rich) Vander Ploeg
Features Editor
The Banner

1 | Always Something

D r. Henry Kissinger is a very wise man. He is a political scientist, a member of the faculty at Harvard University. Sometime ago he showed a little of his wisdom.

He addressed himself to the more hopeful of his fellow citizens who hold the cautious belief that the war in Vietnam may soon be over. He tried to temper their optimism with some realism. "It is a mistake," he said, "to think of peace as some final state of nirvana that beckons seductively somewhere around the bend.

"We have to get rid of the idea that there is some terminal date," he added, "after which we live with a consciousness of harmony."

Dr. Kissinger sought hereby to articulate his conviction that after Vietnam there will be some other problem or crisis; that, indeed, as the years and the decades come, there will always be something standing between life as it is and life as we would like it to be.

Always something! I recall sighing these words already at the age of 10 or thereabouts. The elder who came with the minister for family visitation showed that the generation gap existed then already. Patting me on the head, he said to my father, "If life could only be as simple for us as it is for this little lad." I felt resentment at this. Couldn't he understand that I had worries too—as large to me as his to him?

I recall sitting in the fifth grade, for example, dreading the examination in arithmetic coming up the following week. However, once that was over I would have no clouds on my horizon. But after the test was passed, more or less, there was something else to be deeply concerned about, as my mother announced a forthcoming visit to the dentist. "At least," I thought, "when that is over, I'll have clear sailing. No more concerns." But along about the time of the dental appointment, the lot fell to me, so to speak, to render a piano solo, as the twelfth number on the annual spring program at the church, sponsored by the Men's Society. And so, one cloud merely replaced another. Sometimes there were several. Never were there none. Always something.

I have since discovered that my childhood experience is the history of humanity in microcosm. If only the first world war would end! It did. But it was replaced by the twenties roaring to their Wall Street crash. Then came the threadbare thirties. Surely the forties would be better. Instead, however, they were worse—what with the second world war and the atom bomb. In the fifties we had Korea and Russia's worrisome saber rattling. In the sixties, presently, we have Vietnam abroad and social upheaval at home. Who will say, then, that the seventies will calm the mortal storms? Says the Bible, "There will be wars and rumors of wars." In others words—always something.

"Always something," however, is a line that can be delivered in at least two ways. It can be spoken with a shrug; with drooping shoulders; with the sigh of a fatalist, world weary, longing for the better existence by and by. Such a posture is often equated with high spirituality. There are even some Scripture passages that are cited in its support. It is doubtful, however, whether such a stance reflects

> There will always be something standing between life as it is and life as we would like it to be.

all the light of sacred story. The Christian armor, of which the Bible speaks, would hardly be necessary if all we were called to do is decry the times.

"Always something," then, can be sounded as the Christian's challenge. Standing in the ferment of the years, we must not only look past the present troubles to the times beyond, but at them too. The church must bring itself to bear on matters that try the world today. And when the seventies come, troubled, as all the previous decades in the history of humanity, Christians must know, as Mordecai said to Esther amid the clouds of a more ancient day, that they have been brought to the kingdom "for such a time as this."

(Rev. Eppinga began writing for The Banner *in September 1968. This first "Cabbage" was published November 8, 1968, as part of what was initially planned to be a three-month series of articles.)*

2 | Debut

Last week a friend gave me an old bulletin from my home church. It is dated August 8, 1943. The names in the announcements are familiar: someone is leaving for military service, some are on the sick list, the minister has declined a call, a young lady is seeking room and board, my mother-in-law has broken her arm, a new baby has arrived, the Ladies' Aid will picnic in the forthcoming week on Bob-Lo Island.

At the bottom there is a poem. At the top is the date identified as "The Lord's Day," and directly beneath that it says, "Both services today will be conducted by Mr. J. Eppinga!"

I remember!

It was my first appearance in the pulpit of my home church. Would the guys I grew up with laugh? Pull faces? "A prophet has no honor in his own country" (John 4:44).

I had been preaching for a year in a Presbyterian church in Philadelphia. But this was home! I didn't sleep a wink the night before. When, prior to the service, I met with the elders and deacons, some of whom had been my Sunday school and catechism teachers, I had to excuse myself briefly in order to get rid of my breakfast. I considered not returning.

What did I preach about on August 8, 1943, in my home church debut? I looked into my barrel, but to no avail. Nowadays preachers store their sermons in their computers. Before that, they kept them in files, there to die and rest in peace. Before that, preachers—or so it was said—stored their sermons in barrels. When a minister accepted a call, he just turned over his barrel and started over again. Ha, ha!

Rummaging among my sermonic remains, I could find no messages delivered on what had been a dreaded date. The only thing I remembered were two illustrations: one for the morning dissertation and the other for the evening peroration, both of which went over like lead balloons.

My morning illustration involved Shakespeare's Lady Macbeth, a murderess who, in her sleepwalking scene, sees blood on her hands. She wails, "Out, damned spot! Out, I say!" and then sighs, "All the perfume of Arabia will not sweeten this little hand. Oh, Oh, Oh!"

I have forgotten what that illustration was supposed to illustrate. All I remember is that one of the leading elders—my former Sunday school superintendent—took me aside after the service in order to tell me that the word *damned* in my illustration had been inappropriate. I replied that I could not very well have said, "Out, out, spot," which would have sounded more like ordering a dog to go outside to do his business.

I must confess, however, that the elder had a point. How did it sound in children's ears to hear the word *damned* from the pulpit? As I recall, my motivation in using Lady Macbeth and her sleepwalking scene, though on the mark, was not altogether honorable and commendable. I think I rather enjoyed using a word that would shake up what I then considered a rather stodgy congregation. "Sins of youth remember not."

In the evening I used Mutt and Jeff to illustrate a point. They were my favorite comic-strip characters. Theirs was the first page in the newspaper I turned to—something I don't do anymore, which is a sign that I am growing up.

> I rather enjoyed using a word that would shake up what I then considered a rather stodgy congregation.

In my fledgling years in the pulpit, I often referred to Mutt and Jeff, as comedians in those days referred to Pat and Mike. I found the "Mutt and Jeff" episodes thought-provoking sometimes; their conversations occasionally profound:

Jeff: "I wish I knew where I was going to die."

Mutt: "Why do you wish that you knew where you were going to die?"

Jeff: "Because if I knew where I was going to die, I would never go there."

I think I was trying to say, by way of that illustration, that our times are in the Lord's hands. But after the evening service, another elder took me aside to say that Mutt and Jeff had no place in the pulpit.

Oh well.

Today I tell the famous Dutch story of the gardener who, looking up from his work, saw Death staring at him. Frightened, the gardener borrowed his boss's horse and fled to the town of Ispehaan. Later in the day, the Lord of the manor met Death and asked him why he had come to frighten his gardener.

Death: "I didn't. I was just so surprised to see him here because I have a date with him tonight in Ispehaan."

As often as I tell the story, I think of Mutt and Jeff.

And my debut.

3 | Blue Marble

A man stopped me the other day in a mall. He put his hand in his pocket and pulled out a blue marble. I put my hand in my pocket and pulled out a blue marble. We looked at our marbles, compared them, laughed, and went on our separate ways.

A bystander observing two grown men showing each other their marbles might understandably have wondered whether those two men had lost their marbles.

The story of the blue marble began a long time ago. One of the astronauts on the moon took a picture of planet Earth. Today that picture is well known. It appears frequently in magazines, in books, on billboards. I saw a large reproduction of it recently in a planetarium. I have it hanging in my study in an 8" x 12" frame. The first time I saw the picture, I was struck by its beauty: the earth appears as a blue ball with swirls of white and a few light touches of pink. The blue planet!

Time magazine came out with a full-page reproduction of the photograph soon after it was taken. That's the one I tore out, framed, and hung on my study wall. I contemplate it often. Sometimes when I look at it, I get lost in thought. I think of the One who made it and also of the ones who spoiled it. I am filled with the wonder of it, awed by the sin on it. How incredible that the blue planet stays its course in trackless space! Does God see me as I walk on it? Is he really acquainted with my lying down on it, as I read in Psalm 139?

Once, as I studied the picture, I remembered that I had a marble somewhere that looked like it. Having been a regional marble champion once upon a time, I still had an assortment of leftovers from my marbling days. One of them, Old Bluey, a bit nicked and chipped, bore an amazing resemblance to the picture on the wall. I put it in my pocket. A few weeks later, while casting about for an idea for a children's message for the coming Sunday, my fingers—playing with the blue marble—gave me an idea.

It worked out pretty well. The children came forward, and I showed them my blue marble. I told them about the picture of planet Earth and how my blue marble reminded me of it. I said that God holds the world in his hands just like I hold my blue marble in mine.

Occasionally store clerks will observe that, apparently, I have not yet lost all my marbles.

I said that sometimes I forget about my blue marble, but God never forgets the world. I said that sometimes I lose or misplace my blue marble, but God never loses or misplaces us. I showed them the chip in my blue marble, pointing out that it wasn't perfect. "But," I added, "this isn't a perfect world either, because of sin."

Then we all sang, "He's Got the Whole World in His Hands." I told the children to get a blue marble of their own and put it on their dressers in their bedrooms. It would remind them each time they looked at it that "He's got the whole world in his hands!" The following week, a few children showed me their blue marbles.

Since the world premiere of my blue-marble children's message, I have repeated it for other children in many other churches. Once I did it in the same church twice, by request. And once I told it at a funeral, by request. Today, children here and there have blue marbles. Even some adults do—like the man in the mall.

My blue marble also helps me witness to others. When I make purchases in stores and sort out my handful of change, I make sure that my blue marble is visible among the pennies and nickels, hoping that it might elicit some comment. Often clerks will simply ignore it. Occasionally they will observe that, apparently, I have not yet lost all my marbles.

But when they ask what I want them to ask—"What are you doing with a marble?"—I have them where I want them. Their query is my opportunity. I tell them that my blue marble looks just like the beautiful blue planet on which we live. I say that when I hold it I am reminded that "He's got the whole world in his hands!"

This happened again last week. And the clerk said, "Amen." Wonderful! So get yourself a blue marble. No, this is not a commercial. I am not in the blue-marble business. But if you get one and we meet somewhere, you can show me yours, and I will show you mine. Then we can both rejoice that God so loves the world he made that he not only holds it up but gave it his only begotten Son.

This article proved to be the most popular "Cabbage" Rev. Eppinga ever wrote.

4 | Blue Marble II

As a growing boy I was good at playing marbles in our Detroit neighborhood. One day I entered a marble contest sponsored by the YMCA and won! My father's empty cigar boxes filled increasingly with my growing loot as I played "for keeps." I still have a large tin box with marbles won in that more innocent day.

When a picture of planet Earth appeared, taken from the moon by one of our astronauts years ago, I framed it and hung it on my study wall. I had a marble of similar coloring. Ever since that picture in *Time* magazine, I've carried my blue marble with me. When a store clerk sees it in my handful of change and asks, "Why the marble?" I put it in my other outstretched hand and say, "He's got the whole world in his hands." It's a way to witness—a gimmick to get a spiritual conversation going.

After my article titled "Blue Marble" appeared in *The Banner* some years ago, followed by my book with the same title, I was pleased to note how often, while shaking hands after a church service, people would reach into their pockets or purses to show me their blue marbles.

Sometimes I think about what a lot of mileage I've gotten for my Lord out of what I used to call my "Old Bluey."

The other day, while parking downtown, as I fished in my pocket for a quarter for the parking meter, my blue marble fell out and rolled under the car. A disaster! Retrieving it would make me late for my appointment, to say nothing of messing up my suit in my effort to regain it.

I got down on one knee to see where it lay. There it was! It had rolled under my car to the exact center.

Minds do funny things. When I saw where it lay, Murphy's Law popped into my head. I've memorized quite a few of Murphy's Laws, just for the fun of it. I know God's Law, having read and preached about it often. I've examined Boyle's law in physics and forgotten it altogether. Somewhere between those two extremes, I remember some of Murphy's Laws:

"Anything that can go wrong, will."

"There's never time to do it right, but always time to do it over."

"A shortcut is the longest distance between two points."

"If you try to please everybody, nobody will like it."

"In any hierarchy, each individual rises to his or her own level of incompetence."

"No good deed goes unpunished."

"Where you stand on an issue depends on where you sit."

I have discovered the truth of all those laws, more or less, in pursuit of ministry.

There is still another of Murphy's Laws. It came into my head while peering under my car at my distant marble: "Any coin dropped while standing beside your car will immediately roll underneath to the exact center." That happens with marbles too. I got down flat on my back, reaching with my foot for what had rolled under. A pair of brown shoes appeared and stopped to ask if I was all right.

Me: "I'm trying to reach my blue marble."

As I fished in my pocket, my blue marble fell out and rolled under the car.

Brown Shoes: "You're what?! What did you say?"

Some black shoes appeared and addressed Brown Shoes.

Black Shoes: "Is he all right?"

Brown Shoes: "He wants his marble."

Black Shoes: "You gotta be kidding. What kind of marble is it?"

Some sneakers appeared, embracing growing feet.

Sneakers: "Sir, can I help you?"

Me: "I want my marble."

Sneakers: "Let me get it for you."

And so I learned something more with my marble: "He's got the whole world in his hands. Yes, and never drops it."

Beneath are the everlasting arms!

5 | A Little White Ball

I have just come home from playing golf. I used to think that the game was a waste of time. I had better things to do. Imagine! Grown men and women chasing a little white ball! Today however, you can count me among their number.

Golf gets me out into the wide-open spaces. It is grand therapy for one such as myself, who has spent so much of his life within the narrow confines of a pastor's study. Aren't trees beautiful! And rolling grassy hills! The sky, so big overhead, holds wandering clouds of various shapes and hues. And then there are the birds. Chipmunks. Rabbits. Not long ago, three deer crossed my path, making incredible leaps over a wide water hole. It was early in the morning. I would have missed the sight if I had stayed in bed.

I do not play the game very well. My partner's ball usually goes straight. I use a different system: tacking. Like a sailor, my ball goes left, then right, then left again, and so on, until it reaches its destination. The words of Isaiah often come to mind—something about making the crooked straight.

I used to think that baseball was the only game with myriads of application to life. However, I now find much in the pursuit of the little white ball that brings spiritual lessons to mind. For example, I'm reminded how easy it is to cheat. I played with someone last year who jubilantly discovered his lost ball only inches from the cup. But how could that be when I had his ball in my pocket?

Speaking of lost balls, I usually have little patience looking for them and easily abandon my quest. But as often as I give up, I think of the Great Shepherd, who never stops searching until he has found the one sheep that was lost.

Wandering from right to left, never staying on target, I seem to walk the broad way and not the narrow way of the fairway (few there be who find it). I'm often reminded of the saying "Golf is a game that keeps you humble." After all, golf spelled backwards is *flog*.

> I seem to walk the broad way and not the narrow way of the fairway.

There is a tree where I play my weekly game. Sometimes my ball hits it, and I apologize. Some years ago, playing my first game of the season, I talked to it. I said I was glad I was not a tree. I said I had been here and there the past winter, even to Florida, and all that while the tree had not moved one inch. "It must be boring," I said to it, "to be a tree." Afterward, as I reflected on Psalm 1, I thought there is something to be said for being a tree, especially when the opposite is to be blown about by every wind of doctrine.

My friend H.B. Weijland recently passed away in the Netherlands. He was an eminent theologian, scholar, and churchman who represented his church at our synods on a number of occasions. In his later years he, too, discovered golf—though his small country is hardly large enough to hold golf courses. He was heartsick when someone stole his clubs.

I'm glad that, in his lifetime of dedicated service, the Lord allowed him to find the pleasures of chasing a little white ball.

6 | Why Me?

I have a kidney stone. It's my ninth. Some people never even have one. Not fair! Why me? The X-ray shows I have another one incubating in my left kidney. I ask you again, "Why me?"

I've heard it said that we're all born equal. Baloney! The fact of the matter is that some are born with silver spoons in their mouths. Others are born with seeds that will turn into kidney stones. Like me.

There is an inequality built into all creation. Some fish are bigger than others. Some trees are taller than others. A moth lives a day and an elephant 70 years. One star shines brighter than another. Some people are given five talents. Others two. Some only one.

There is inequality in heaven too, where he who is least will be greater than John the Baptist. Jesus said so (see Matt. 11:11).

But there's something wrong with the question "Why me?" It's the essence of complaint. It implies that if I have nine kidney stones, all people should have the same amount. It forgets that other people have problems too. Some greater than mine. It's a self-centered question and, ultimately, an accusation against God. So what must I do with my question?

I can turn it from "Why me?" into "Why not me?"

There is so much unhappiness in the world. Millions of people go to bed hungry every night. Why not me? The evening paper's daily ration of misery—people robbed or killed or buried in mudslides or kidnapped or drowned in a giant tsunami—is too much. I turn to the sports page. But when I focus on the tragedy rather than turn the page, I often ask, "Why not me?"

I've lived a long time. I haven't been everywhere, and I haven't seen everything. But as a pastor I've been exposed firsthand to some things I could have done without. Neglected children. Broken homes. Murders. Suicides. Painful deaths.

So much agony has passed me by. Born into a Christian home with loving parents. Warm houses. Three square meals a day. But so many do without any of those blessings. Why not me?

There is a second thing I can do with the question "Why me?" I can turn it into a hymn of praise and thanksgiving.

> In his weakness he asked, "Why me?" But it was not his ill fortune he had in mind.

I prize my doctor as a physician and a fellow Christian. When I saw him last week and told him I had yet another kidney stone, I added, "Why me?" He told me the story of Arthur Ashe.

Arthur Ashe was an honorable man and the best tennis player of his day. He conquered Wimbledon! A skinny black kid from segregated Richmond, Virginia, he grew up to become No. 1 in the world. But in 1988 he received the overwhelming news that he was HIV positive, having contracted the AIDS virus through a tainted blood transfusion.

He died in 1993, a great humanitarian who did much to combat apartheid in South Africa. In his weakness he asked, "Why me?" But it was not his ill fortune he had in mind. Instead, he was thinking of all the great blessings in his life.

Thanks, Doc. I needed that. I too can ask "Why me?" when "nothing in my hands I bring." I too can ask "Why me?" when "'twas not so much that I on Thee took hold, as Thou, dear Lord, on me."

7 | Little Things

Why do so many people race each other to the next red light, only to bide their time there and repeat the contest all over again the split second the light turns green? Why are we in such a hurry? "Speed kills," says a sign on a wall in the local police station. But driving under the speed limit—a rarity—is almost as dangerous.

A police officer stopped a lady for driving 18 miles an hour in a 30-mph zone. "I was going the speed limit," she said, pointing to a sign that said "18."

"But lady," responded the officer, "that is a route number. Before I let you go, tell me, why do all your passengers look so frightened?"

The lady behind the wheel explained, "They'll be all right in a minute. You see, we just got off Route 92."

For years I traveled Route 92. That is to say, I had a heavy foot. Arriving at a new charge in a strange town, I yelled "Tortoise!" at a slowpoke in front of me. I'm thankful he didn't hear me, since he turned out to be not only a member of my new flock, but the treasurer.

I still get a bit impatient with slowpokes in front of me, but nothing approaching road rage. As a matter of fact, I have well nigh cured myself of inordinate haste while sitting behind the wheel. Nowadays, whenever I find myself stuck behind a snail, I say, "Thank you, Lord, for putting that crawler in front of me. Without him holding me up, I might get a speeding ticket or experience something worse—like maybe an accident."

Have you ever considered how an unwelcome delay spared you from something worse? The tragedy of Sept. 11 brought an end to many lives. But some were spared through little things:

The head of a company came in late that day because his son started kindergarten.

Another was spared because it was his turn to buy doughnuts.

One woman was late because her alarm clock didn't go off on time.

One was late because he got stuck on the New Jersey Turnpike because of an accident.

One missed his bus.

One spilled food on her clothes and had to take time to change.

One person's car wouldn't start.

One went back to answer the telephone.

One had a child who dawdled and didn't get ready for school as soon as he should have.

One couldn't get a taxi.

One had a pair of new shoes that pinched him, causing a blister, so he had to stop at a drugstore to get a Band-Aid.

So perhaps when I'm stuck in traffic behind a crawler, it is because God has me exactly where he wants me.

What an influence little things can have, not only on people but on history. Robert Bruce, the George Washington of Scotland, pursued by his enemies who sought his life, took refuge in a cave. As soon as he entered it, a spider began to weave its web across the entrance. His pursuers never examined that cave because, as they said, "If Bruce was in it, the web would have been broken." And so Robert Bruce—and Scotland—was saved.

For want of a nail, a shoe was lost. For want of a shoe, a horse was lost. For want of a horse, a rider was lost. For want of a rider, a battle

Have you ever considered how an unwelcome delay spared you from something worse?

was lost. For want of a battle, a war was lost. For want of a war, a country was lost. And all because of the loss of a nail? Such a little thing?

Is Providence involved in all of these little things? Read Lord's Day 10 of the Heidelberg Catechism and ponder. It says, "Providence is the almighty and ever present power of God by which he upholds, as with his hand, heaven and earth and all creatures, and so rules them that leaf and blade, rain and drought, fruitful and lean years, food and drink, health and sickness, prosperity and poverty—all things, in fact, come to us not by chance but from his fatherly hand."

Lord's Day 10 is the one Lord's Day of the catechism that I have the most trouble with when, say, I must bury a little girl hit by a car. I do not doubt the doctrine of Providence, but even in the little things? It is too deep for me. But I'd rather have this doctrine than be without it.

Meanwhile, why not read this article over again before you go out. It will delay you only five minutes and, who knows . . .

spare you from being hit by a meteor.

8 | The Bishop and the Quaker

It was a meeting of ministers. They all loved the Lord. But I found their conversations excessively peppered with such expressions as "Amen," "Hallelujah," and "Praise the Lord." It was, in my opinion, greatly overdone. But, feeling the pressure, I began to speak their language. Then I stopped. I wasn't being me. It was not the way I talk. I was praising the Lord and "amening" to impress my colleagues. Wrong. I thought of Samuel Hobart.

It happened long ago in England, during the reign of William III. One of the bishops of the Anglican church wanted some of the chairs in his banquet hall repaired and some new ones added. He wanted nothing in his palatial surroundings to appear shabby or second-rate. He was, himself, a man of elegant taste. His personal appearance was always impressive, his ecclesiastical garb elegant. His aides and servants were always properly deferential. He was, in short, everything befitting his station as a bishop in the church.

The best furniture establishment in the city was owned and operated by Quakers. Their manners were quaint. They removed their hats for none and called all people "friend." They had been persecuted, but now they were tolerated. Mr. Hobart, owner of the furniture firm, received a summons from the bishop, who wanted nothing but the best. Mr. Hobart was to come the next morning to consider the bishop's request for new chairs and for the refurbishment of the old ones.

The next morning it was not Mr. Hobart—who was out of town— but his assistant John Evans who appeared at the bishop's behest. The bishop's servant, properly attired and disdainful of the Quaker visitor, bowed to his eminence and said, "M'Lord, may I present to you Mr. John Evans."

Young Mr. Evans, keeping his hat firmly on his head, and without bowing, cheerily greeted the bishop and said, "Good morning, friend."

> Hobart had never yet had a bishop for a customer.

The bishop, who had never seen a Quaker before, thought to himself, "So this is a Quaker. I have heard that they do not remove their hats in greeting others, all of whom they address as 'friend.' He is not very deferential. Even my wife addresses me as m'Lord. This young fellow, on the other hand, doesn't even bow."

John Evans explained that his boss, Samuel Hobart, was out of town on business and that he had come instead to discuss the matter of the chairs. He took measurements. Yes, the existing chairs could be refurbished. They could also be duplicated. "How much will it cost?" asked the bishop.

John Evans replied, "I cannot tell thee that, friend, until I discuss the matter with my employer. Friend Hobart returns on the morrow, and he will let thee know."

"Excellent," said the bishop. "I shall count on it."

The next day John Evans told his boss about the request from the bishop. "The bishop!" exclaimed Hobart, "I hope your demeanor was a proper one." Hobart had never yet had a bishop for a customer.

Evans saw the concern in his boss's face. "I greeted the bishop as we greet all people, as an equal and with respect."

Hobart was distressed. He went directly to see the bishop. As he approached the cathedral grounds, he practiced little bows. He wondered whether his eminence should be addressed as m'Lord or as Your Grace.

Meanwhile, inside the bishop's palace there was a meeting of state officials. The bishop was telling these honorable gentlemen about John Evans, the Quaker. "I admire those people," he said. "John Evans would not remove his hat, nor bow, addressing me as 'friend'—all in keeping with his principles—although he must have been under some pressure to compromise his ways in my house. The young man's boss is coming today. You must observe him when he comes and you will see what I mean."

As he was speaking the bishop's servant approached, bowed, and announced the presence of Samuel Hobart. Samuel approached from the far end of the room, bowing and scraping. He stammered "M'Lord," then quickly corrected his greeting to "Your Grace." His hat was in his hands.

The state officials hid their smiles from the embarrassed bishop. The bishop said tersely, "Please send your man John Evans. I'll do business with him."

Hobart realized that he had badly misjudged. He retreated from the room in confusion. But the bishop, a softhearted man, followed him to the door. He said, "Mr. Hobart, you are a Quaker. Be one, and do not be intimidated to be what you are not."

And so Mr. Samuel Hobart, Quaker, learned a lesson from the Anglican bishop, for the bishop was right!

Amen?

9 | The Brothers

L eonardo da Vinci (1452-1519) was a total genius! He was a painter, a sculptor, an architect, a musician, an inventor, an engineer, a botanist, an astronomer, a geologist, and an anatomist. He had a knowledge of aviation far beyond his own time. He painted the famous *Last Supper,* which is considered to be one of the greatest paintings in the world.

Recently in our town there was unveiled a huge twenty-four-foot-high statue of a horse. It towered above all those who had come to behold its first appearance. It was built from sketches and designs by da Vinci. What a man!

And yet . . .

One day the counselors of Florence, Italy, asked Leonardo to submit sketches for the decoration of the city's grand hall. One of the counselors had heard of a young and little-known artist—a fellow named Michelangelo—and asked him to submit some sketches too. Those of Leonardo were superb. But when the counselors saw those of Michelangelo, there was a spontaneous expression of wonder and acclaim. His sketches were chosen.

The news reached Leonardo, along with a remark of one of the counselors: "Leonardo grows old." Da Vinci was never able to get over being eclipsed. He filled his remaining years with jealousy. Wow!

Jealousy, it is said, is the sin of the "have-nots." Wrong! It can also be the sin of the "haves." As a sinner, I have dealt with it in myself. As a pastor, I have dealt with it in others. I have observed it as the one sin that, absolutely, has no pleasure attached to it. It is a cancer that, if not nipped, can eat the soul.

There is an old Jewish story that can moisten the eye. Once upon a time there were two brothers. One was single. The other had a wife and three children. Together they owned and farmed a piece of land. Such co-ownership is often rich soil for the growth of jealousy. Such was not the case with these brothers.

They were not afraid of work. They bent their backs. They put their shoulders to the wheel. In time they were rewarded with a rich harvest. They mowed. They reaped. They bound the wheat in sheaves. Then they divided the sheaves equally. Half were placed on one side of the field for the single brother, while the other half were placed on the other side for the brother who was married. Then they retired to their respective dwellings to rest for the night.

At midnight the unmarried brother awoke and thought, "Oh, how selfish I have been! My brother has many mouths to feed and needs more sheaves than I." So he dressed, went out into the night, and moved three of his sheaves to his brother's side of the field. Satisfied, he went back to bed.

An hour later the married brother awoke and thought, "Oh, how selfish I have been! My brother has no children. When he grows old, he will have no one to care for him. He should have some extra sheaves so that he can have some extra savings for his old age." So he arose, went out into the night, and moved three of his sheaves to his brother's side of the field. Satisfied, he went back to bed.

> Jealousy, it is said, is the sin of the "have-nots." It can also be the sin of the "haves."

The next morning, to their amazement, the brothers saw that the sheaves were still equally divided. Neither one said anything. The next two nights the little drama was repeated. Again, with equal results. On the fourth night they ran into each other. Then they understood why those sheaves had remained equally divided despite their efforts on each other's behalf. They laughed. They embraced.

People in the Bible who suffered from jealousy—people such as Cain, King Saul, and Judas—could have profited from this ancient rabbinical tale. So could Leonardo. So can we.

10 | Deep Purple

"The next century will be all genetics, as this one was all physics." That's what the expert, while being interviewed on my car radio, said. He spoke of altering DNA of millions of human fertilized eggs in banks everywhere, of cloning Abraham Lincoln from his hair molecules, and more. I found some of his projections frightening. If even half are true, theologians, among others, have much to ponder.

Of course, this century hasn't been all physics. In its earliest years there was Luther Burbank, a plant breeder and horticulturist who devoted his life to developing the Burbank potato—to say nothing of creating new trees, fruits, flowers, vegetables, grains, and grasses. By crossing and by selection he originated a number of fruits and vegetables of commercial value. Did you ever sink your teeth into a Burbank pomato?

But not only was there a Burbank in the earlier years of this century. In its closing years, there is me and my extensive experimentations with the hydrangea—a handsome shrub in the saxifrage family.

It all began with a beautification project. In its pursuit, my wife and I sought to enhance the appearance of our front yard. At considerable expense we had seven hydrangea plants installed. Already in the first year our septuplets grew healthily to full maturity. But, alas, the flowers were white! The mistress of the manse had set her heart on purple blooms. That's when the experimentations began.

A neighbor, whose name is not Burbank, suggested putting some nails in the ground. The man in the hardware store gave me a funny look when I asked for the best nails he had for hydrangea plants. With a smirk, he asked if my plants were broken. Ha, ha!

I drove a dozen of his best spikes into the ground around each plant. This treatment of the earth, I was told, would alter the soil's composition sufficiently to turn white blossoms to purple in the following season. Baloney! The following season, the blossoms were as white as ever.

The problem was obvious. Not enough nails! I pounded more of them into the ground. By the dozens.

> The mistress of the manse had set her heart on purple blooms. That's when the experimentations began.

A friend laughed. Was I trying to hold the world together with nails, having failed to do so with sermons? He laughed some more. A comedian! But, smugly, I knew I would have the last laugh. The following summer my flowers would turn purple.

When they didn't, I just about did! Consternations!

I sought the advice of an expert. "Coffee grounds," he said. He knew about all things of a horticultural nature. With the help of used coffee grounds, he predicted, the flowers would turn a deep purple. There was a song by that title. I kept humming it as I fed my hydrangeas coffee grounds. Decaffeinated, of course! No sense keeping them awake at night.

Someone in church heard about my efforts and began saving her used coffee grounds for me. She is a member of a large family circle, all of whom drink coffee morning, noon, and night. Hooked on the bean! She gave me a large plastic bag filled with 15 pounds of grounds. Marvelous! My wife and I increased our own coffee intake. We were drowning in oceans of it for the sake of our hydrangeas.

All seven septuplets are now standing root deep in a field of java outside our bedroom window. We can awaken each morning to the smell of coffee—grounds, that is!

When it's time, will the emerging flowers be purple? What a lot goes on in gardens! Eppinga and his hydrangeas . . . Burbank and his potatoes . . .

Adam and his apple!

11 | Sequel

The June 8, 1998, issue of *The Banner* contained my article titled "Deep Purple." It was about my hydrangeas. I had been trying to change their color from white to purple. I had been advised to sink nails around their roots. Others suggested coffee grounds. Alas, neither the one nor the other, nor both together, succeeded in altering the color of my flowers. They blossomed forth, as ever, white as could be, fulsome and beautiful.

What surprised me was the response my article elicited. In an ongoing sort of way, I receive a modest number of calls and letters regarding many of my articles—but nothing compared to what happened after I wrote about my hydrangea experiments. I didn't realize how many *Banner* readers are hydrangea experts. The phone rang off the hook. I received letters from Florida and California and Alaska and many places in-between.

I learned more about hydrangeas than I wanted to know, including the fact that in the Dutch language they are called *hortensias*. Did you know that for pink flowers you need gobs of phosphorous in the soil? And aluminum for blue? For the latter, an application of alum phosphate is best when applied in September at the rate of 15 pounds in 100 gallons of water! The trouble is that I do not have a 100-gallon tank. I asked for one for my birthday, but I was given a tie instead.

The most discouraging letter, from a local source, told me that my hydrangeas will stay white no matter what I do. This is what I read: "Make sure you have hydrangea *macrophilla hortensis*. Do not bother with the white hydrangeas, or snowball (viburnum). They stay white no matter what you do."

45

Ah's me! All those nails and coffee grounds for nothing.

I thought about Old Testament Jacob. He made a bargain with Laban, his father-in-law (Gen. 30). Jacob proposed that Laban give him all the speckled and spotted animals from his flocks as wages for all the work he had done. Jacob would then tend the remainder of the flock and would keep for himself any speckled or spotted that might be born to the normally colored animals. Laban promptly agreed to this proposal, which was so favorable to himself. If Jacob was so foolish as to suggest such an arrangement, let Jacob suffer the consequences.

But Jacob was no fool. He took branches from trees and made white stripes on them by peeling the bark and exposing the white inner wood. He then placed these branches in the watering troughs. The animals, staring at the striped rods every time they quenched their thirst, thereby produced offspring that were speckled and spotted. It is the story of one knave outwitting another. So Jacob grew prosperous while Laban gritted his teeth.

This story, recounted here all too briefly, raises a question in my mind. If Jacob Israel could put speckles on sheep, why can't Jacob Eppinga change the hues of hortensias?

Of course, even Jacob Israel had his limitations. Although his "genetic engineering" could put spots on the offspring of spotless animals, he could not, I am sure, do the reverse and remove spots from leopards or their progeny (see Jer. 13:23). It is as impossible as changing the color of my hydrangeas. So I am told.

Our Lord, however, can do the impossible. He who ordained that neither my hydrangeas nor leopards can change their appearances

> I didn't realize how many Banner readers are hydrangea experts.

can change human hearts radically. He changed Saul into Paul. And how about Bill?

Bill was a friend of mine. He died years ago. He was vile in appearance and vile in heart and soul. It was as impossible to change him as it is my hydrangeas. And yet before Bill died, God changed his heart. God clothed Bill "with garments of salvation and arrayed [him] in a robe of righteousness" (Isa. 61:10). God changed him—not with any chemicals but through the blood of Jesus Christ.

Wonderful!

12 | Love Is Kind

Paging through my pastoral record the other day, I came across the name of J.N. He died almost 20 years ago.

J.N. was small of stature, with a white brush on his head and a very aristocratic mustache under his nose. Though humble and gentle of manner, there was, nevertheless, something patrician about him. I was not surprised when I discovered that he was of noble birth. He showed me his family coat of arms. It was one of his few possessions.

He needed a new suit and a new pair of shoes. Meanwhile, his old suit and his old shoes bore evidence of meticulous care. Few were poorer, but also, few were better groomed. It was also true that few were as lonely. He had never married. What relatives were left were far away in the old country.

Spying him in my new congregation one Sunday morning, I determined to make a call on him that following week. He was pleased when I made an appointment with him after the service. He specified only that I come in the evening, and not during the day.

I found him on the top level of a downtown building whose middle floors were all vacant. In a room overlooking the main street below, he was seated at a huge rolltop desk. It seemed to be a doctor's office. J.N. wore a green eyeshade in the manner of bookkeepers of years ago. He said that he had been charting the stock market developments of the day. Suspenders crossed his back over a neat white shirt, while behind him, on shelves lining the wall, huge bottles of medicine stood starkly and lonely as sentinels, circa 1900. It was indeed a physician's office.

"I live here," he said. "I sleep in the waiting room on the chairs." I sensed that I should receive this information as matter-of-factly as it was imparted. I had noticed reed chairs in the anteroom on my way in. He probably put several of them together for sleeping. But how could he manage even forty winks that way! I thought of my own comfortable mattress at home and felt sorry for my friend.

He opened a quart of milk and a bag of cookies. He had bought them for the auspicious occasion of my visit. Sharing these, he told me more. He was a sort of night watchman for the doctor. At nine each morning he had to be out, for then the doctor came in. That's when he went to the Exchange Building to watch the stocks each day.

Before I left, we had devotions together. He manifested a firm Christian faith and a deep thanksgiving for all his blessings. When I retired that night, I saw him in my imagination lining up four reed chairs. I went downstairs and lined up four kitchen chairs and lay down on them. But only for a minute. What a way to sleep!

Several months later I received a phone call from a certain Dr. B. Could he come to see me about an urgent matter? That afternoon a man who appeared to be 70 but who, in reality, was much closer to 90, strode into my study. He came to the point quickly. Did I know a certain Mr. J.N., who was a member of my congregation? Perhaps, being new, I had not yet met the man in question. I told him that I had made his acquaintance. "A fine gentleman," I said.

"Indeed he is, but he is also my problem," said my visitor. "Years ago I befriended him. He had so little and I had so much. I asked him to be my night watchman, though, frankly, I didn't need one. But, at least, it gave him a place to lay his head. I also paid him a small

> It was time for him to have a nice bed instead of four reed chairs.

weekly sum, and I still do. I even let him be my stock consultant on occasion—for a fee. But I warn you, beware of his advice.

"All this started 20 years ago when I had a practice. He was always out of the office in time. The patients in my waiting room never knew that someone slept there at night. He kept the place neat and clean."

My visitor continued. "Reverend, today is my 88th birthday. For several years now I have longed to close my office and retire. I have no patients left, even though I still come to the office every day. I just sit there and read and while away the time and keep an office going for the sake of J.N. But, really, what I have wanted to do for a long time now is go to Florida. If that is ever to happen, it had better be soon. But I can't go anywhere so long as I have J.N. on my hands."

Dr. B. leaned forward. He was coming to the point. "Could you suggest to him, without involving my name, that it is time for him to find a retirement home? I am willing to contribute to the expense involved. But, please, do it gently. I wouldn't want him hurt, not for all the world."

"What a wonderful man," I thought, as I showed him out.

Soon thereafter, I made my way to the doctor's office again. J.N. sat there as before, wearing his green eyeshade. The stock market had dipped that day.

As gently as possible, I broached the subject of my mission. It was time for him to find a retirement home. It was time for him to have a nice bed instead of four reed chairs.

In answer, I heard a tale of love similar to the one I had heard from Dr. B. He was, indeed, too old to sleep on chairs. But the doctor needed him. So long as that need was there, he would stay, though, truthfully, it was getting harder and harder on his bones.

With the help of the deacons of the church, a change was finally made. J.N. loved the Holland Home. "Feel the bed," he said to me. After I had admired its softness, he showed me a nice card. It was from Dr. B.—from Florida.

13 | Of Batteries and Silverware

I was young, impressionable, and attending my first Christmas Eve service. It was 11 p.m. The cathedral was filled to capacity. The view from my first-row seat in the balcony seemed to lift me from this world to the next. The only source of light was from countless candles flickering in the nave, alongside the aisles, and around the stone pillars. The robed choir, processing down the center aisle, was joined in the singing of "O Come, All Ye Faithful" by the standing worshipers, of which, thrillingly, I was one.

Coming from my background of plain Christian Reformed Sunday services in which choirs were not yet permitted, I couldn't believe that worship could be mingled with such beauty. The clergy, in their multicolored robes, followed the choir. The last one, walking alone, looked like a white-haired Old Testament prophet. The members of the cloth ascended the steps at the front and took their respective places. The hymn ended. As we remained standing, transported in spirit, all hearts aglow, one of the lesser of the clergy approached the lectern and solemnly addressed us all. He said, "There is a green Chevrolet in the parking lot with its lights on." He gave the license number.

Alas! The heavenly spell was broken! What a letdown! My soaring spirit plummeted to earth with a thud. I had expected to hear words like "The Lord is in his holy temple" or "Glory to God in the Highest," but "There is a green Chevrolet in the parking lot with its lights on"? You've got to be kidding!

I remembered a visiting clergyman in our own church back home when I was a youngster. I was impressed with his ministerial aura. When the prelude ended, he strode impressively to the pulpit, gazed lovingly upon us all, paused for effect, and then delivered his opening words: "Please remember the church picnic next Saturday, and don't forget to bring your own silverware." He emphasized the word "silverware" as though it were one of the five points of Calvinism. Ever after, I've always thought of him as Reverend Silverware.

> Alas! The heavenly spell was broken!

Why couldn't they have ignored that green Chevrolet? To maintain a Christmas mood inside was certainly worth one dead battery outside. Was this the devil's way of breaking the Yuletide spell? Why was the owner of that Chevrolet so careless, anyway? A battery's death on the night of Christ's birth was surely preferable to an interruption of the Christmas celebration. Any and all convocations in church, I concluded, ought never to begin with references to car batteries or picnic silverware. Phooey! I found myself unanimous in my opinion.

❦

I went to our church recently to hear an organ concert. I was excited. The organist was the world-renowned Carlo Curley. The sanctuary was packed! I couldn't wait! Precisely on the hour, Mr. Curley appeared. He was accompanied by one of our organists who no doubt, and with appropriate deference, would introduce this musical giant who was in our midst. I cupped my ear so that I would not miss a single word. Greeting one and all, our organist said, "There is a white Chrysler outside with its lights on." He gave the license number. I looked with widened eyes at my wife. Consternations! It was OUR car!

It was kind of humiliating to have to get up amid so many of my fellow church members. I tried to avoid their laughing eyes. But wasn't that nice of someone to report this matter to our organist? And wasn't that kind and considerate of him to announce it?

Just think! We could have had a dead battery!

14 | The Lonely

There is a program on public television called "Waiting for God." The person I live with says that it is a bad program. Sacrilegious! I never watch it. As a matter of fact, I never watch television. Ever.

"Waiting for God," I am told, is the story of some people who live in a retirement home. They are old and, as they say, "on the shelf." They have nothing to do all day but wait for death; hence the title of the program, despite the fact that the principals in the drama—supposedly a comedy—don't seem to believe in God at all. So I am told.

However that may be, homes for the aged hold my special interest. There are three "rest homes," as they are called, in the area where I live. I visit all three every week. It's my work. It's what I do. And I have been doing it long enough to know that not all the residents I visit are waiting for God. But just about all of them are waiting for visitors and friends. That's where I come in. Because that's what I am—a visitor and a friend.

It is true that not all the residents of the rest homes I visit like to see me coming. But those who will have nothing to do with me are a distinct minority. Most of the residents are happy to see me, and I am happy to see the expressions I bring to their faces.

Alas, I have never learned to drive, and so the person I live with furnishes my transportation. Arriving at my first stop, I always take a deep breath of fresh air fragranced by the beautiful flowers that grace the main entrance. I wish that those inside could do the same. Then I enter and make my rounds and brighten people's faces.

The first to greet me is the lady in the wheelchair with the doll in her lap. The nurse says that I'm the only one who can make her smile. The man in room 27 is always reading. He used to be a professor. He dislikes being interrupted. But when I come close, he closes his book and pulls gently on my ear. The lady across the hall always wants me to get in bed with her, and I oblige.

In the next room is the man who always rubs me the wrong way, but he means well. In the room across the hall is the cracker lady. She always saves them for my weekly visit—a whole week's supply. To please her, I swallow hard every Tuesday. I'm not much for dry crackers, but eating them always makes her look so very pleased. My reward.

And so it goes. I touch many lives each week and, in the process, have developed a special feeling for the very lonely. Some residents have daily visitors, but others see none at all, like Mrs. B. She is very refined in her manners. Her hair is always in place. But I never see any callers in her room, and I never see any flowers. She has a bird feeder outside her window. I overheard the nurses talking about her one day. They said that they, the birds, and I were her only friends. But she has her dignity. She told the nurses that she has a loving son who lives in Florida and would come if he could, but he can't. She says he calls her every Sunday afternoon. Faithfully! Poor thing! The fact is, the nurses say, her son never calls, and she hasn't heard from him for a very long time. That is beyond me.

There is another old mother in the rest home I visit on Wednesdays who is equally lonesome. I have learned that she has a son in town who never fails to call on her—every Christmas. Hard to believe!

She has a son who never fails to call on her— every Christmas.

If I could, I would write about this and speak about this and tell people, some of whom are so concerned about the "heathen" in lands far away, to remember those who, by blood and distance, are much closer to them— their own aged parents, uncles, and aunts. But I can't preach about this because, well, let me introduce myself.

My name is Fido. I am a dog. One lady calls me her golden retriever, which I am not. I'm just a mutt. But when I let her rub my fur—even if it's the wrong way—she smiles and says that I help her retrieve golden memories of yesterday. Nice.

Lord Byron—although not the greatest of characters—called me and others of my kind "Man's best friend." But that's not me. That's Jesus. Meanwhile, I'm glad that I can bring some happiness to some people. One lady said that it's wonderful that God made beings like me. She said that I ought to have my collar turned around, like her pastor's. Wow! Nice compliment!

But now I gotta go. My third rest home for the week is my favorite. It's got a fire hydrant by the curb.

15 | Canine-ology

No, *The Banner* is not going to the dogs. Just this page. Being partial, I've long thought of paying my respects to these creatures God has made.

Why are these animals so devoted to the human race? They delight in our company and, unfailingly, welcome us home. We do not have a dog at present, but I still owe a debt of gratitude to Spotty and Pal, who brightened the days of our family life as long as we had them.

How many Christian Reformed dogs are there? Our denominational yearbook doesn't say. Pal should be in it. She always knew when it was Sunday and never left her box in the kitchen corner when we had family devotions.

Years ago I had a book I should have never loaned out because I never got it back. Its title: *Prayers of Animals.* I saw it in a bookstore. I flipped through it aimlessly until I came to a page titled "The Prayer of the Dog." That's when I bought it and took it home. The prayer? "O Lord, only you and I know what faithfulness is."

Moya is one of our granddogs. A German shepherd. A one-man dog. She waits by the window when it's time for our son to return home from work. When Dick is out of town on business, she waits in vain. But when he calls later in the evening from wherever he is, Moya is allowed to hear her master's voice. Then Moya licks the phone.

While canvassing the neighborhood some years ago, I was bitten by a dog guarding a house. I had a bone to pick with its owner. And once I called on a young couple who had the biggest Saint Bernard you ever saw. It drooled hugely, its enormous head resting on my lap while I prayed. Nor did I mind another time when a dog used me as a tree.

One question I have dealt with more than any other in my ministry always comes from the littlest people: "Will there be animals in heaven?" They're thinking of their beloved pets, mostly dogs. I never feel any biblical warrant for answering in the negative. After all, if Paradise Regained means the Paradise that was, it should be remembered that the Paradise that was, was full of animals.

I still owe a debt of gratitude to Spotty and Pal.

Speaking of heaven reminds me of my favorite dog story. There was a Christian physician whose office connected with his house. Meeting patients, he had merely to step through the door from his living quarters to his place of practice. He made a strict rule that was to be unfailingly observed by his children and his dog. They might never spill over into the office when Father was busy with patients. Sometimes the children forgot. But Rex never did.

One day a patient who was terminally ill called on the doctor. This man loved the Lord and was assured of his salvation. Nevertheless, he harbored some fears about his coming death. What would it be like? The doctor prayed with him. But before he did, he opened the door leading to his living room.

The doctor said, "I have a dog, Rex. She has never come through that doorway, but now I'm going to call her." He did. Rex appeared, stopping short of the threshold. The doctor coaxed Rex to cross over. She would not. She had been trained well. Finally, after several minutes of urging, she took one flying leap and landed in the doctor's lap.

The doctor turned to his patient. "This is what it's like," he said. "Like Rex just now, death is like going where you have never been before. But it's all right . . . because the Master is there."

16 | Jelly Beans

At the posh reception the groom beckoned me to a corner. It was apparent that he had important business with me.

"Thanks for tying the knot," he said.

"You're welcome," I replied. Thereupon he produced an astonishing bank roll and importantly peeled off two one-dollar bills. A third, tentatively removed, quickly rejoined a disappearing wad of twenties. "Here's something for your trouble," he said.

Driving home with two whole dollar bills for my effort, I fell into a laughing jag. He had been so solemn about it! I imagined a man sitting on a mountain of sugar, carefully dispensing two—almost three—grains of it. At a stoplight, a driver in an adjoining car shot me an apprehensive glance. He seemed concerned about my apparent lack of sobriety. In a gale of laughter, I gusted away, leaving him far behind.

The next morning a man came to my study. He said he was down on his luck. I gave him the two dollars. As he pocketed the money gratefully, the amount suddenly seemed much larger than the night before. Then, suddenly, a memory came to mind. I sat down and dusted it off.

❦

It was an Easter weekend of long ago. Just about everyone had gone somewhere, leaving me pretty much alone. It was too far to go home, and so I stayed at the seminary. Anyway, I had no money. A few nickels. A few streetcar tokens. That was about it. A check would be arriving on the forthcoming Monday. Although that was a comfort, it hardly solved the problem of eating in the meanwhile. Clearly, here was a matter to test my mettle. After all, Easter was hardly the season for fasting.

Obviously, the first thing to do was to call Mrs. Appleton. She was the supervisor at the Methodist Seamen's Home. She had called the seminary earlier in the week for a student to preach for the Sunday-evening meeting. She paid two dollars. I had appeared there once before and it was the hardest two dollars I had ever earned. No one listened.

Mrs. Appleton was delighted. It was so dear of me to volunteer. She hadn't really blamed any of the students for not calling back because, after all, it was a holiday. But how noble of me to be willing to sacrifice! After more such compliments, I hung up, feeling guilty. At the same time, I had my physical needs for Sunday evening provided for. With two dollars I could go to Horn and Hardarts. I liked their ham and cheese on poppy seed rolls. My mouth watered. I turned my attention to Sunday noon.

I decided that I would worship at the Germantown church. Someone there might invite me to dinner. It had happened before. Little daunted by the fact that both my Sunday morning and evening religious exercises were being planned around my stomach, I turned my attention to my more immediate need. It was still Saturday morning—a long way to go to Sunday noon and someone's dinner table.

I decided to walk to Glenside, a small town at a little distance. Mr. Johnson, a Greek, at whose establishment I frequently took my meals, would be most sympathetic. If I promised to pay him on Monday, he would surely "put one on the bill" for me. As I waited to see him,

Driving home with two whole dollar bills for my effort, I fell into a laughing jag.

I absentmindedly inserted one of my two nickels in his pinball machine.

It was a strange thing to do. I didn't approve of those things because they paid off. I could have used the nickel for a candy bar. Nevertheless, there I stood pulling on the knob. Before Mr. Johnson could appear, I had won sixty-five cents. It was just enough for the special of the day.

The attendance at the service the following morning was swollen by those invisible creatures who materialize biannually in churches each Christmas and Easter. Listening to the minister, and looking him up and down, I thought he looked well fed. Meanwhile, the little boy directly ahead turned around to see who was sitting directly behind with such a noisy stomach. It would have been more Christian of him to offer me a peppermint. After all, he had three left.

After the service I greeted everybody once, and half the congregation twice, in an effort to wangle an invitation. The crowd, fast dwindling, I grew confused. Approaching an elder, I inquired solicitously after the health of his aged ham, when I meant his aged father. I considered looking hungrily at the lady with the cook look, but feared she might misunderstand. Having had nothing to eat since the previous noon, it now appeared that my agony would be even more prolonged.

That evening Mrs. Appleton viewed my gauntness as monastic and spiritual. But the service was dismal. Behind a family of four, deputized by a local church to help with the singing, a dozen or so men preferred the chairs along the walls to those neatly arranged. One sat on a table. Another played solitaire. Mrs. Appleton played the piano. The visiting family sang. I saved what strength remained to me for the sermon. The vision of two dollars helped me to my feet.

Halfway through my second point, a crisis arose. It is amazing what reserves of strength are available even to the weak. A drunken sailor entered at the back and, spying a spittoon to the left of him, proceeded to relieve himself. The telltale sounds registered unmistakably on my first row family. With poise and admirable restraint not one of their faces turned. On the contrary, each reddening, was the more riveted on my own. Mrs. Appleton was the least composed, while I was equal to the challenge. I began to shout and thunder, drowning out the competing sound. It was there I learned to raise my voice in preaching.

After the service I received my reward. Dear Mrs. Appleton! She said she usually paid two dollars. But it being a holiday and all, she had decided to go all out. She gave me a lovely Easter basket instead, complete with bunny. Going home on the streetcar, sitting in the back, spent from preaching and bent from hunger, I gave the basket to a little boy with big brown eyes.

Someone once told me unkindly that I preached for money. It is not true. The only time I ever did, I got jelly beans instead.

17 | My First Picture Show

Thats's what we called the movies. My playmates always went on Monday evenings with their parents because it was a free-dish night, and it was the Depression. My parents, unenticed by free dishware, never went because we were Christian Reformed. Synod had decreed against movies, card playing, and dancing. My friends came home from the picture shows and told me about Tom Mix, famous cowboy, and Rin Tin Tin, famous dog. It sounded interesting. Still, going to picture shows was sin.

The first movie I saw was on a ship. We were sailing to Europe to visit relatives. My father took me to the evening entertainment, which turned out to be a film. Before falling asleep, one scene stuck with me—and has to this day. It was a boy's bedtime. He was told to brush his teeth. He wet the toothbrush under the faucet and replaced it in its holder. What a neat trick! A clever deception! When we were home again, I, too, held my toothbrush under the faucet and put it back. I deceived my parents. It was a sin. I learned it from the picture show. Synod was right to banish such things. I was only 5 and already influenced for evil.

My first real picture show, however, was one I went to see all on my own when I was in my teens. It was a Western. A close friend of mine had gone to see it—which was all right because he was Lutheran—and urged me to see it too. He said that it was a piece of Americana. A true depiction of frontier days. It made our country's history come alive.

I was persuaded. I put on an old hat, pulled the brim down to eye level, looked furtively up and down the street, had the right change ready in hand, and darted in, conscience-stricken. I heard the voice of my minister: "What if you died in a theater?" But his words faded fast as my eyes focused on the screen. I was transfixed. It was all so real. I remember it quite vividly. There were

> I was only 5 and already influenced for evil.

the bad guys and the somewhat good guys. I identified with the latter and despised the former. Then—oh, no!—one of the good guys was shot dead!

They buried him on Boot Hill. Just outside of Dodge City. Then, mind you, they found some twigs and made a cross and planted it on the grave. Then the leader, who had a weather-beaten face, spewed forth some tobacco juice. They called it "tobaccy." He removed his bullet-riddled hat, looked up into a deep sky, put his hand over his heart, and offered a prayer not at all like our minister in church.

He said, "Well, Lord, this here Gus was an ornery critter. But then, ain't none of us much good. Gus here shore was no saint. But, Lord, you said somethin' nice once to a crook on the cross. Mebbe you could say somethin' nice to Gus too. Mebbe he can hear. Thank ye most kindly." Then he replaced his excuse for a hat, mounted his horse, spat some more tobaccy, and rode off.

I was shocked. Synod was right. This was no place for me. That was no prayer. It was playacting, and it was sacrilegious. I almost walked out. I would have, but I was hooked on the story and wanted to see how it all turned out. But today I often replay that prayer scene of my first picture show in my head and think about it. I consider it significant. Let me explain.

Synod eventually lifted its ban on movies. Now that they are mostly 10 times worse, we can all go. And I do—on occasion. And I watch movies on television—on occasion. And I notice that whenever there is a burial scene, there is usually some clergy member who speaks some appropriate words from the Bible or from the Book of Common Prayer. It is as if, in the presence of death, when those of the world have no words to speak, they borrow our words of life. They borrow our book—a book they never read themselves. Interesting. The world thereby unwittingly proclaims that when dealing with death, Christians possess something that the world doesn't.

Over the years I have had many requests to baptize babies of unbelieving parents. I decline but use the opportunity to witness. I've also found that many who have never darkened church doors still want church weddings, which I don't decline. The same goes for funerals—a church "setting" is desired by many who never engage themselves in church "sitting." In fact, there are those who go to church only three times in their entire lives: when they are hatched, matched, and dispatched.

A pity!

18 | The Burning Bush

She was dividing her attention between the sermon and her children. With the former less interesting and the latter more demanding, it was clearly my message that was losing out. After the service she spoke to me in the manner of a martyr.

"I'll be glad when they're grown up." With instant recall, I remembered a day, to my regret, when I had expressed a similar wish.

✽

Our daughters were still too small, but our two sons were clearly approaching the age when they could replace the baby-sitters we hired upon occasion. It was our persuasion that they had taken what small tasks we had assigned them with a creditable sense of responsibility. Clearly they were ready for more. Accordingly, when an occasion arose that called us away for an abbreviated evening, we announced that the time had arrived. For a few hours they would be on their own.

Leaving enough instructions behind to fill a small manual, we waved good-bye to four hands in the window. Feeling as though we were going abroad instead of just a half-dozen blocks away, we were already considering cutting a short evening even shorter. Arriving at our destination, the first thing we did was call home.

Everything was fine. But not yet two hours later we were the first to leave—to the regret of our hosts. Returning, we found four angels. Two asleep. The two who were awake were unusually responsive to our hugs and to our directives that they should immediately retire. Slipping behind my newspaper, I had the wonderful feeling of a father who knows that all is right and wonderful in the world of his little family.

❦

The next morning it all came out. First with reluctance and hesitation. Then in a torrent, as both sons interrupted each other continually to supply us with all the horrible, ghastly details.

Shortly after our phone call, the boys had begun to play with their homemade rubber gun. Shooting kitchen matches from the second-floor window, they aimed them at the brick side of our neighbor's house. The object was to make the matches ignite on impact. It had been fun to see the brief light in the darkness before their "bullets" fell extinguished in the snow.

But a mishap had occurred. One of the ignited matches had rebounded into a nearby bush under the neighbor's window. It was soon in full blaze, just like that bush in Moses' day. There had followed a race to the kitchen for pans of water and repeated trips to the burning bush.

"But didn't anybody see anything of this?" Though I was beside myself, I managed to ask the question. It was then that we were given more to comprehend—if this was possible.

After the boys had returned to their window to make sure all was quiet and under control, the fire department had arrived. Neighbors

> After the boys returned to their window to make sure all was quiet and under control, the fire department arrived.

came out of houses. Men stood in small knots, talking and gesturing. Four small eyes, peering from behind drawn drapes, surveyed them all. After a while, the people went away, including the big red truck.

✖

Having digested what was really indigestible, we told the boys to go to our neighbor with their story. Mr. Brown was an amiable sort, a pipe-smoker whose love for kids was exceeded only by his love for bushes. "Tell him you will replace that bush," I shouted after the receding figures, "and remember, it's coming out of your allowances."

Later that morning I sauntered over myself. I say "sauntered" because I tried to manifest a calmness I didn't feel. "Funny," said Mr. Brown, "I was reading my newspaper with my back to the window, but I noticed flashes of light even though the curtain was drawn. I told my wife that I couldn't ever remember having had lightning in January."

"But what about the fire department?" I asked. "A neighbor called them," said Mr. Brown. "Firemen are good people," he added. I agreed. I was trying to be as agreeable as possible. I figured I was hardly in a position to be anything else.

"But they are not perfect," said my neighbor. Recognizing this as a sound piece of theology, I again gave my full assent. "They couldn't find our street. They took off in the wrong direction and they went all around the lake." Mr. Brown was referring to a small body of water a half mile to the north. "All the chief could find was what looked like prints of barefeet in the snow. Small. Led to your house. But I said you weren't home. All the lights were out."

Mr. Brown relit his pipe. "I'll let you know about the bush. I know just what I want." I made a mental note to look up a catalog on bushes. Were they expensive?

⁂

Home again, my wife and I had a cup of coffee. That's when I said to her what the lady had said to me in church. But it was a spur-of-the-moment statement. I'm sorry I ever said it. That's why I answered the lady in church as I did:

"Don't say a thing like that! Yours are the golden years. When your children are grown, you will find yourself thinking back with nostalgia to the days when they were small."

As she moved away I thought back—to finger marks on walls. Toys in the middle of the floor. Baths and busyness on Saturday evenings with work still waiting in the study after bedtime stories. Wonderful! So, if there are any who read these words against a background of children's voices, singing or crying, enjoy—enjoy! Children are a heritage from the Lord. Happy is the one who has a quiver full of them (Ps. 127:5).

Only make sure their own little quivers contain no matches.

An Eppinga family favorite

19 | It Could Be Worse

A aron Levi said that he'd had it. Bringing his hand up to the level of his throat, he said he'd had it "up to here." He added, "It couldn't be worse."

Aaron Levi and his wife and four children were living in one room. The baby cried all night. There wasn't enough space, and there wasn't enough food. Aaron Levi couldn't find work, and his savings were gone.

It couldn't be worse.

Aaron Levi went to the rabbi for some advice. It was in a day when all rabbis were considered to be men of great wisdom. The rabbi listened patiently to the recitation of woes that Aaron Levi climaxed with his characteristic expression, "It couldn't be worse." After a long silence, in which the rabbi pondered Aaron Levi's plight, the rabbi said, "Buy a goat."

Buy a goat? What strange advice! But Aaron Levi did what the rabbi said. The rabbi, after all, was a man of wisdom. Alas, Aaron Levi's woes increased. His situation deteriorated from impossible to doubly impossible. He shook his head. He said, "It couldn't be worse."

Aaron Levi went back to the rabbi. He said that the goat had greatly multiplied his problems. The goat was eating what little food was left—the canned goods, including the cans. The goat was relieving himself in the corners of the room and all points in between. The stench was unbearable. It just couldn't be worse. What should he do?

The rabbi listened patiently to Aaron Levi's recitation of woes. After a long silence, in which the rabbi pondered Aaron Levi's plight, the rabbi said, "Sell the goat."

Aaron Levi sold the goat. Thus he learned that his original plight, to which he had now returned, could have been worse. The rabbi had cured him of his monotonous refrain.

I thought of this classic story last Sunday on my way to a preaching date. I always arrive in plenty of time. I hate being late. But someone had kept me on the phone too long, giving me a late start. The traffic was heavy. All the stoplights were red. To top it off, I had to wait for a train. Woe was me! I looked at my watch with alarm. I had visions of filled pews and an empty pulpit. "It couldn't be worse," I said to myself.

But I was wrong. The train could have been switching back and forth, as trains have a habit of doing. Or it could have been crawling. As it was, the train was gaining speed with every second. It could have been worse.

Watching the disappearing train, I pursued my own train of thought. I remembered the man I had recently called on who was very sick. He moaned and he groaned. I sympathized. I said something about how it couldn't be worse. But the man corrected me. He said, "Considering the alternative—death—it could indeed be worse." I wondered, Why do some Christians say that, when Paul said that to be with Christ is far better (Phil.1:21)?

I checked to see if I had my sermon with me. I might have forgotten it in my rush. But there it was. It could be worse. I might have been without it. It was about Job. He was bad off. It couldn't have been worse for him. Wrong! Things would have been far worse for him if he had not believed and, therefore, could not have said, "I know that my Redeemer lives" (Job 19:25).

Buy a goat? What strange advice!

Habakkuk had it right. Things couldn't get worse. The poor were being oppressed. The Babylonians were coming. But, he said, even if the fig tree did not bud and there were no grapes on the vines, even if the olive crop was a failure and the fields were barren, and even if there were no sheep in the pens and no cattle in the stalls, he would still rejoice in God (Hab. 3:17-18).

Things could be worse.

It is better not to complain to God all the time and tell him that things couldn't be worse. You might get his goat. I mean, he might put one in your living room.

I made it to the church on time.

It could have been worse.

20 | The Preacher Factory

I visited ours recently. Calvin Seminary. The present emphasis is on better preaching. Good! God is not boring! Let's not make him so.

Today's seminarians are more mature and more often married. They have a computer room where they sit and stare at screens. In my day we were younger and less married. We pawed through concordances. We called our school the "Preacher Factory."

I was a lighthearted student. Perhaps because I had not yet wholly committed myself to a future ministerial career. There were a few kindred spirits along with me on the assembly line who were also in search of God's will for their lives.

The professors? There was Cornelius Van Til with his pre-suppositional apologetics. He was given to preaching on downtown street corners in Philadelphia with me and my trumpet in tow. I tooted. He addressed the passing parade. He asked me to assemble a male quartet for his 6 a.m. program on radio. I couldn't find a tenor, so I assumed that role myself. Mistake! I wasn't a tenor. I couldn't reach the high notes. Even on tiptoe. And certainly not at 6 a.m.

There was Professor John Murray, the dour Scot. Yet not dour at all if you knew him. Standing before us in class, lecturing deeply on dogmatics while adjusting the window shade to admit more light into the room—if not on his subject—the whole thing came crashing down on his head. Unperturbed, and with no interruption, he went right on lecturing. Three minutes later, after he'd made his point and adjusted his papers, he "came to," as they say. Staring at the offending shade on the floor, he kicked it with surprising force across the room, as if trying for a field goal. What fun!

There was Professor Paul Woolley, a walking train-schedule manual, who asked us in a surprise test to sketch the life of St. John Chrysostom. My friend, P.T., caught flat-footed, drew three pictures: Chrysostom as a child, as a man in his prime, and as a graybeard.

> For a time we almost lost the art of ordinary prose.

If the professor wanted a sketch, P.T. would give him three.

For some reason, a few of us fell to speaking Shakespearean. My sketching friend, addressing me in a loud voice as we strolled down the avenue, would say, "See'st thou yon mortal with balding pate?"

My reply: "Nay, sire, behold rather approaching lass with flaxen curls."

For a time we almost lost the art of ordinary prose.

Hitching a ride home to Detroit, I was dropped off late in the evening on the seamy side of downtown Toledo, Ohio. With but a paltry sum in my pocket, I was forced to rent a room in a fleabag motel. No lock on the door! In the night I sensed an unwelcome presence in the room. Without forethought I bounded to my feet on the mattress, bounced wildly up and down, and screamed, "Gather thy dignity about thee as a shroud and go forth to the reprehensible doom of thy destiny!" It was like the intruder vaporized. He was gone in a flash.

Are you disappointed in this rather one-sided report on seminary life? Forsooth! Desist! It was a place where I saw students from fundamentalist backgrounds discover with delight what had been my heritage all along, namely the Reformed faith. Something I had taken for granted.

Most of my classmates are now gone. They are with Jesus. But turned loose in the world they became preachers, teachers, evangelists, missionaries, professors, seminary presidents, theologians, authors, and chaplains, some of whom lost their lives in combat.

All soldiers of the cross. Let many who come after them follow their steps and enter . . . a preacher factory.

21 | Fabrication

I am seeking a friendly lady who belongs to a wire-haired terrier. I owe her an abject apology.

It all began, innocently enough, with Dick and Judy going away and leaving their dog in our care. "Shadow" is friendly, obedient, and very Christian Reformed. At least, when the Bible is read for devotions, at table, she lies respectfully still. She is also a good walking companion and, further, arresting in appearance. People especially notice her long hair. As with a 1947 Studebaker, they cannot tell her front from her rear.

Each morning and evening we both looked forward to our walks together, which we enjoyed, disagreeing only on where she could leave her calling cards. With her hairy face and eyes completely hidden, I felt a little like a seeing-eye man. Still, it was Shadow who spotted the terrier before I did, and the friendly lady at the other end of its leash.

"Hi," she called, smiling brightly from across the street. It is wonderful, I thought, how easily dog owners converse. With canine icebreakers, they are unlike ships which pass in the night. I read of a fellow once who "rented" a dog just so he could meet the young lady in the park where, each evening, she walked her own. And I remember two preachers who were on no speaking terms whatsoever. Having split a theological hair, they had become members of opposing camps and, well—enemies. There was no principial possibility of their ever speaking again. But one morning, walking their dogs, they met. It was not the first time that tables were turned, in that it was a dog that got a man to "speak." Indeed, two dogs got two men to speak, rather than bark at one another. Surely a dog is a man's best friend!

"Hi, yourself!" I was equally cordial to the friendly lady who was now following her dog in my direction. "What kind of dog is that?" She addressed me as if we were old friends.

I was about to say that Shadow was a mixture, which, indeed, she is. She came from Tobermory in Ontario, Canada—supposedly an old English sheep dog. When it became apparent, as she grew, that she had other blood in her—something having gone unaccountably awry, as her breeders said—Dick and Judy had their money cheerfully refunded. Before I could answer, however, Friendly Lady spoke again. "I've been watching your dog for a block, and I can tell, even by the walk, that she is a purebred and, though I say it myself, I'm never wrong."

I couldn't find it in me to contradict Friendly Lady and tell her that she was, in fact, dead wrong—that Shadow was more like a mutt. So I simply said, "Sheep dog." I said it proudly. It was really no lie, I thought. It was, indeed, half true. Yet, that was my mistake. The rest of the conversation was all downhill for me.

"But it's not an Old English—I can tell by the plume of the tail!"

So she did know her dogs! What was I to say next?! The whole truth? But that would certainly deflate Friendly Lady! She was so nice, so self-assured! Amazing how many thoughts can flow through the brain in just a split second!

In the following split second, I spoke. "You're right! Not Old English! She's a Shropshire sheep dog." Where that word "Shropshire" came from so fast I haven't the foggiest, unless it was the devil who put it on my tongue. It was an English word, and it sounded just right. I

> **If you read this, Friendly Lady, forgive me. I made the same mistake Abraham made.**

repeated it again, meanwhile wondering where Shropshire was—if, indeed, it was a place at all.

Friendly Lady was delighted. "I just knew it wasn't Old English, though I was sure it was a purebred. But I must confess I never knew Shropshires. Thank you for telling me."

"Not at all," I said, feeling quite miserable by this time. Then, unaccountably and quite unnecessarily, I dug the hole I was in still deeper. "You can always tell a Shropshire by the plume of its tail and by its friendly disposition." At this, Shadow turned and looked at me with hidden eyes.

The next day we walked around a different block.

I wish to make amends. If you read this, Friendly Lady, forgive me. I made the same mistake Abraham made when he told Abimelech that his wife was his sister. What he said, like what I said, was half true because she was his "half" sister (Gen. 20:12). But half-truths always become whole lies. Preachers, too, like the father of believers, need to remember that they must tell the truth, the whole truth, and nothing but the truth, not only in courtrooms, but on streets.

And in their pulpits too.

An Eppinga family favorite

22 | All Creatures Great and Small

What a lot of animals there are in the Bible. A regular zoo! One could almost tell the whole gospel story in their terms: from creation and the naming of the animals, through the Fall and the serpent, to the new world in which the wolf shall dwell with the lamb and the leopard with the goat (Isa. 11:6). Being partial to dogs, I was always pleased, as a boy, that they befriended poor, lonely Lazarus (Luke 16:21). And happy, too, that people in those days remembered to feed them table scraps (Matt. 15:27).

How impoverished life would be if God had not made the lower creatures! It would create a big dent in children's literature. I still love my book *Black Beauty*, the story of a horse, given to me when I was 10. No child should grow up without *The Wind in the Willows* by Kenneth Grahame. C.S. Lewis always kept a copy of this animal story on his bed stand along with the Bible. Nor should any boy or girl grow up in ignorance of Ernest Thompson Seton and his perceptive stories involving animals. And how about Lassie? Or the writings of Lewis Carroll, whose walrus spoke of cabbages and kings? I can't count the times I have told the story of *The Three Bears*—although never to adults. Children and animals go together. If we love the former, we shall remember how they love the latter. But so do many grown-ups. Read the books by James Herriot.

I'm glad that the Bible is not silent on the subject. It is true that Samson's cruelty to animals is reported without commentary. And so is David's. Tying foxes tail to tail (Judges 15:4) and hamstringing horses (2 Sam. 8:4) are certainly not the best things these ancient luminaries ever did. People who beat animals should read Numbers

22:28 to see what the lower creatures would say if they could speak. But kindness to animals is directly commanded in Scripture. We must help the overloaded beast of burden (Ex. 23:5), respect the birds (Deut. 22:6), help the ox in trouble (Luke 14:5), and, altogether, as Proverbs 12:10 says, "Care for the needs of [our] animals."

How impoverished life would be if God had not made the lower creatures!

Alas, if the king of beasts could read those words of Solomon, he would shake his mane sadly over how far we have parted from the Bible in this respect. He would recall the decimated herds of buffalo on this continent and of elephants on another. Walter de la Mare, author of *The Huntsman*, wrote:

Bang! Now the animal

Is dead and dumb and done.

Nevermore to peep again, creep again, leap

again,

Eat or drink or sleep again, Oh, what fun!

At the time of the flood, God saw to it that Noah built his boat big enough to save the animals from extinction. When I was small, my father, who kept as many animals as he could on our small city lot, said there was a lesson in that. Many, however, have not learned it, as laws must be passed to save the whale, the eagle, and many other endangered species. The North American Indian, a hundred years ago, said, "I sing for the animals." Charles Darwin, whose name is not readily invoked on these pages, was kindred in spirit as he said, "Physiological experiments on animals is justifiable for real investigation, but not for mere damnable, detestable curiosity."

The SPCA (Society for the Prevention of Cruelty to Animals) should have the strong support of every Christian. In a sinful world, there is cruelty to children. There are battered wives and aborted lives. There is so much that requires prayer and care that it seems silly to some to take a page of this publication to make a plea for lower creatures. Even so, if God cares for them, as we are told in Psalm 104, so should we. We don't have bullfights in our country, but what about such rodeos as are insensitive to animals' feelings, and fairs, where catching greased pigs is great sport? And what about those seal hunts in the north, where clubs wielded by men sink with sickening thuds into skulls, and where some of the animals, only wounded, lumber away to suffer and die?

What about thousands of good, upstanding citizens who drive into the country to "lose" a pet they no longer want? And what about factory farming? Behind the neat packages of meat, eggs, and milk in the stores are farm animals that often lead miserable existences. How many laying hens live their whole lives in cages where they can't even stretch their wings? Under unnatural conditions, many die of acute stress. Hogs and beef cattle suffer too from many modern "improvements" that step up production. Some veal calves are kept in total isolation in places so narrow they cannot turn; they are fed deficient diets and suffer anemia for their four-month lives because they taste better that way. There are those in the industry who are sensitive to these matters. There are more who are not.

Albert Schweitzer was known for his respect for all life. He wrote a prayer for animals, especially those who are lost or deserted or frightened or hungry. In it he asked that all who deal with animals might have a heart of compassion, gentle hands, and kindly words. "Make us," he wrote, "true friends to animals, and so to share the blessings of the merciful."

All creatures great and small—the Lord God made them all.

An Eppinga family favorite

23 | A Rambling Conversation

We talk a lot. Sometimes briefly. Sometimes far into the night. About everything under the sun—and above it.

Recently, being avid fans, we were talking baseball. We were in my car. I was driving. I said that, in my opinion, Pete Rose belonged in the Baseball Hall of Fame.

He: I disagree completely. He was an inveterate gambler. His private life was nothing to write home about. What kind of example would it be for young Americans if we put such a man on a pedestal in baseball's holy halls?

Me: (Not seeing the light turn from red to green and being prodded by an angry horn behind us.) I see your point, of course. But if character is the measure for entrance at Cooperstown, then I can think of many ballplayers who ought to be nominated for the Baseball Hall of Fame because of their unsullied reputations, despite the fact that they couldn't throw, catch, run, or hit. And what about Babe Ruth? He was certainly no paragon of virtue. A drunkard and a womanizer. Still, nobody would dispute his place among the gods of baseball.

≈≈≈

We had arrived at my house, but the flow of our conversation was uninterrupted. We wandered wordily from ballplayers to other subjects, and then, for some reason, to Hollywood stars.

He: What I said for Pete Rose goes for some Hollywood stars too, like Woody Allen. He may be gifted, but in his personal life he certainly colors outside the lines.

Me: (Reaching for an article on my desk.) Funny you should mention him. I just happen to have this article about him. He was recently interviewed in London by Nigel Farndale, a reporter. Woody Allen spoke to him about his fear of death. Let me read what Mr. Allen said:

> We agreed that it would be good to say a prayer for Pete Rose and Woody Allen.

"You find you are happy with a lovely wife and only then do you realize what is in store for you—it is going to end somehow. You are going to die. . . . When I go for a walk in Central Park on a beautiful day, I have to set myself mental tasks—prepare a speech, think about casting. Otherwise I know I will want to run up to people and shake them and say, 'Why are you bothering to sunbathe? What is the point of your pregnant belly? Why are you walking your dog?' . . . I will look around the park and think, 'We can cut to the scene 100 years from now, and all these people will be dead. Every 100 years a big toilet will have flushed and a new group of people will be in their place.'"

He: How sad. Woody doesn't have the gospel.

Me: Do you ever think like that?

He: No. Do you?

Me: Sometimes I wonder.

He: And you a preacher? A doubting preacher?

Me: One of my favorite texts in the Bible is, "Lord, I believe; help thou mine unbelief" (Mark 9:24, KJV). I take comfort in the fact that Jesus didn't excommunicate right on the spot the man who said that, who expressed his weakness. I must confess that those words are sometimes my prayer.

He: And does the Lord answer you?

Me: Whenever I pray those words it seems that the Holy Spirit leads me to contemplate the resurrection. That really happened. A historical event. Just like "In 1492 Columbus sailed the ocean blue." That puts me on course again. Restores my faith. And chases the devil away.

We talked some more about Woody Allen. He reminded us of Jean-Paul Sartre, the existentialist, who said that life was meaningless and that the only logical thing anybody could do was to commit suicide. And we spoke of Albert Camus, the existentialist novelist, who died years ago in an automobile accident in Africa and who once said, pensively, that he wished that Christianity were true, but it wasn't. Sad. He too agreed with Sartre.

It was time to end our talk. Before we did, we agreed that it would be good to say a prayer for Pete Rose and Woody Allen and all those who live in darkness. And so we did.

The above rambling conversation took place in my head. *Me* is me. And *He* is also me.

Surely, I'm not the only person who talks to himself.

24 | Grump

From September 2007 to May 2008, Rev. Eppinga invited "C.R. Mouse"
to fill in writing "Cabbages and Kings" for him. Though several hints were
dropped, many Banner *readers remained confused as to who the mouse*
really was. It was Eppinga himself.

Chaucer spelled my name *mous.* In Latin it is *mus.* The
influence we had on that dead language is well-known.
Edimus, Vivimus, Biblimus, Oremus, etc. Be that as it
may, there is a man in our church whose moniker is far
more apt: Mr. Grump! And that is what he is—and does.

Being grumpy all the time has permanently twisted his face like
that of a man with a lemon in his mouth. Indeed, some people call him
"Sourpuss." I mentioned him once at one of our mouse conventions,
which we call "Inter-Nos," and from the response, discovered that
every church has at least one.

Mr. Grump mostly grumps about the sermons of our pastor. They
are too deep or not deep enough. Too long or not long enough. He
calls the short ones "sermonettes" and always adds, "They're for
Christianettes."

The only time he laughs, and that derisively, is when he says, "If
the preacher's text had a cold, the sermon never caught it." The other
thing he says every Sunday is, "The preacher missed the central
thrust of the text completely." *Ad nauseam!* Paul had a thorn in his
flesh (2 Cor. 12:7); our minister has Mr. Grump.

To counteract Mr. Grump, some members came up with the idea
of having a Pastor Appreciation Sunday. It took some work, some
meetings, some committees, including a refreshments committee

(goody!) to get the idea off the ground. A retired minister was engaged to deliver the sermon. He chose his text from 1 Thessalonians 5:12-13: "Now we ask you . . . to respect those who work hard among you, who are over you in the Lord and who admonish you. Hold them in the highest regard in love because of their work."

> Paul had a thorn in his flesh. Our minister has Mr. Grump

I didn't record the sermon, but I remember some of it. Among other things, the visiting preacher said that those Thessalonians needed to be reminded—as we all do—to hold our pastors in high regard, even though they cannot walk on water and sometimes spill on you while serving spiritual food. He told the people to remind themselves that the human race is not made up, as some believe, of three classifications: men, women, and preachers. He said that if people are entitled to one idiosyncrasy, preachers are entitled to two.

He went on. The most important words in any language are "thank you." People should remember that preachers also have feet of clay, and that if they preach too long they should still be called "Reverend" and not "Neverend."

He pointed out that "pastor" is the better designation, and how it derives from "parson," meaning "person"—in olden days "the person" in the community. He didn't like it that even children these days address pastors by their first names—a sign of the times. And another—namely that some ministers are released from their positions for insufficient reasons—like the way they comb their hair.

I thought it was a good message, and I hoped that our minister felt the love the congregation expressed by way of that special service.

Everybody was there, including Mr. Grump. His comment on the sermon by the retired minister was overheard by all when the refreshments were served. He said:

"He missed the central thrust of the text completely."

25 | Cheap

It was time to find a motel. Why drive in the dark and miss the scenery? The motel I found, part of a nationwide chain, looked too expensive. The mom-and-pop establishment across the street looked cheap. I turned the wheel toward the latter.

Being a child of the Great Depression, I still operate under the motto "Cheaper is better." Anyway, why choose a more expensive facility when all you plan to do is close your eyes to it all and sleep? I signed in. The price was right.

I had hoped to read myself to sleep, as is my custom, but there was no lightbulb in the lamp! I called for one. Why would it take so long to bring one lousy lightbulb? When it finally appeared, I was no longer in the mood to read my book.

In the bathroom I discovered the complete absence of any toilet paper whatsoever! Another call. Another wait. I sat down in a chair. It fell apart. It had been a nice chair once upon a time, but the glue in all the joints had dried out and let loose.

When I checked in, I'd noticed a sign on the ice machine: "Out of Order." I didn't stop to think that everything else in the place might be out of order too. I deposited myself on the lumpy mattress and listened to the all-night drone of trucks. "Next time," I thought, "I'll choose a more expensive place."

But I never do.

Like I said, I'm a child of the Depression. I can still hear a neighbor, who had his fingers in all sorts of pies, say to all his friends, "I can get it for you wholesale!" He was a popular fellow. Why do I think back to those days so often? Probably because living in the past is cheaper.

I remember a car my friend and I bought for $5. We had 17 flat tires on a 50-mile trip. I also remember a $40 Overland. It used a lot of gas, and more oil than gas. I was penny-wise and pound-foolish. But I had no choice.

> "Next time," I thought, "I'll choose a more expensive place."

They say that Franklin Delano Roosevelt's alphabet-soup projects pulled America through the Depression. So did a sense of humor. The country's poorest days sparked its best humor. Remarkable! They spawned the Jack Bennys, the Fred Allens, the Milton Berles, and others, with all their "cheap" jokes. They said Jack Benny was so tight that when he winked, his kneecaps moved. Fred Allen's wife wanted to see the world, so he bought her a map. And Milton Berle believed that a friend in need was a friend to avoid. A whole nation laughed, and understood, when a radio comedian said that he wanted to die with his boots on because he had holes in his socks.

Although the cheap jokes are no longer in vogue in this time of plenty, when fewer of us travel through life economy class and more of us first class, we still go for bargains. We fall all over each other in the stores the day after Thanksgiving to get in on the sales. It's part of the human condition. Thomas Paine said that what we obtain cheap, we esteem too lightly. Wrong! I think of the man who showed me his new secondhand car. He looked ecstatic when he told me he got it cheap. "A steal," he said.

By all of which I want to make a point. Opting for a cheap motel is no sin. Opting for cheap grace is.

Dietrich Bonhoeffer, executed by the Nazis, climbed the steps to the gallows in Flossenburg, Germany, on April 9, 1945. Before the trapdoor was sprung, Bonhoeffer, brave and composed, said a prayer. Bonhoeffer's attendant said that he hardly ever saw a man die so completely submissive to the will of God.

Bonhoeffer was a theologian. His most famous book was arrestingly titled *The Cost of Discipleship*. Think about it! In it he wrote about "cheap grace"—the preaching of forgiveness without repentance, without commitment, without discipleship, without the cross.

Bonhoeffer addressed those who, in the words of the hymn, would "be carried to the skies on flowery beds of ease." But why would we wish that? I remember another hymn, sung by an old man with a strong voice in a small gathering where I preached. I copied the words. I have them in my Bible. A sample:

> *By and by, when he holds out his hands,*
> *Welcoming hands, nail-driven hands,*
> *I'll wish I had given him more.*
> *More, so much more,*
> *More of my life than I e'er gave before.*

No cheap grace.

26 | Fighting the Devil

I recently demoted an old sermon of mine to file 13. I had preached it long ago for my examination into the ministry. I had kept it in a prominent place for more than a half-century as a reminder of how not to preach. I thought it was about time to lay its yellowed pages to rest. As I did so, it brought some memories to mind—and some reflections.

⚶

I was being examined for entrance into the ministry of the Christian Reformed Church. I had to preach a sermon for the church fathers on a text of their choosing and submit copies in writing. The text they chose was taken from John 1:14: "And the Word was made flesh and dwelt among us, and we beheld his glory, the glory as of the only begotten of the Father, full of grace and truth" (KJV).

A great text! But, alas, my circumstances severely limited my time for sermon construction. In order to stretch it to a decent and impressive length, I threw in a thorough lambasting of modernists (liberal theologians) who denied the truth of that text. I took them to the cleaners! In my oral rendition, I engaged the enemy with vigor and demolished him.

My hearers were not as impressed as I had hoped they would be. My sermon critics told me, and rightly so, that it was all very well to duel with the devil, but I had veered from the central thrust of the text. There were other biblical passages, they said, that were more suited to that purpose.

Having failed to distract my inquisitors with my fervent orthodoxy, I could hardly tell them that I had thrown in a dose of apologetics to make my sermon the required length.

The rest of my examination, I fear, was equally underwhelming. If I had been one of my examiners, I might have voted against me. But in the end, and after meeting in executive session, they let me in.

> I think it was the cigars that did it.

I think it was the cigars that did it.

I had been up the whole previous night awaiting the appearance of our firstborn. When he finally announced his arrival, there was barely time for me to drive the 150 miles in my oil-leaking hack to that ordeal known as my classical examination.

Considering my mood, my lack of rest, and my dubious preparation for a most important event in my life, I deemed it prudent to stop on the way to buy several boxes of cheap cigars wherewith to soften my interrogators as well as to celebrate my new fatherhood.

I had already preached in a dozen Christian Reformed churches, and I had noticed that all their consistory rooms were smoke-filled. I imagined approaching all those present with a gift: "Have a cigar. Have two." I gave to all out of my largesse. During dinner hour it was satisfying to see the chairman of the day chewing on my stogie.

"Sometimes a cigar is just a cigar." Who said that? And who said, "What the country needs is a good five-cent cigar?" Well, what I needed was to pass that examination. And I did! As I already observed, I think it was the cigars that did it.

❦

Remembering that old sermon, I regret to this day that I marred it with an unworthy motive. I am grateful to this day for those sermon critics of long ago who were sharp homileticians. The long-saved pages of that sermon served as a constant reminder to take out of a text what is in it (exegesis) and not to put into it what is not in it (eisegesis).

But they also served a further purpose all those years—namely as a reminder to use the pulpit for combat. Not always, of course. Sermons are for instruction, comfort, and inspiration. But they are also for engaging the enemy. I am afraid that there is a diminishing emphasis on the latter in churches across the land. I pray that people of the Reformed faith will always remember that theology matters.

I had a disconcerting experience sometime ago. Receiving an invitation to preach, I submitted my Scripture selection, sermon title, and the songs I wished sung. The closing hymn of my choice was "Onward, Christian Soldiers." I was asked to change my selection on the grounds that it was too militant. I looked for a substitute. But as I did, I thought of that old hymn in the blue book of some years ago:

Am I a soldier of the cross? . . .
Are there no foes for me to face?
Must I not stem the flood?
Is this vile world a friend to grace,
To help me on to God?

⋯⋯

Passing my classical examination, I was ordained. The officiant read from the formulary. I was charged to "strengthen [the flock] against all error," to "contend earnestly for the faith," to "reject every doctrine in conflict [with the Scriptures]." I was told to be a "guardian" and "a good soldier of Jesus Christ."

Agree? If not, can I persuade you with a cigar?

Just don't smoke it!

27 | Two Pastoral Calls

O nce upon a time there lived a minister in a small European village. There was much poverty and privation there, for the times were bad. Some managed better than others. There were the faithful who observed the day of worship, and there were the others—men, women, boys, girls—who spent their time in idleness and in much drinking.

The minister did what he could to raise the spiritual and cultural life of the place, but with little success among those outside his flock. Indeed, he was resented by them, especially by the young ruffians who frequented the local tavern—hooligans all!

Late one stormy November night there came an urgent knocking on the parsonage door. When the pastor's wife answered she was informed that a parishioner who lived at a distance was gravely ill and asking for the preacher. The minister's presence was urgently requested. The messenger at the door quickly disappeared into the night.

The pastor dressed hurriedly to call on the member of his flock who lay, presumably, at death's door. With his battered lantern and a stick he made his way slowly through the inky darkness. The cutting wind extinguished the useless flame in his lantern. He probed carefully ahead with his stick before each step. Once, then twice, his foot sank into a bog that he knew he must avoid at all costs. In the oppressive darkness he also feared the nearby canal, which meant certain death and a watery grave if he miscalculated his steps. Cold and wet from weather and perspiration, he knew he was in great peril.

After hours of struggling through the night, he thought he could make out the dim outline of the humble dwelling of the stricken member of his small congregation. He approached the door and knocked. Several minutes passed before someone answered, for all within had been sleeping soundly. To his surprise, no one knew anything about an urgent message for the minister. He was invited to step inside. A fire was lit to warm him and to dry his clothes. The wife of the supposed patient—who was himself the picture of health—made coffee and pancakes. After the storm abated, the minister went home again.

Twenty-five years went by. The minister, now elderly, was still at his post, for he loved his people dearly.

One evening a messenger came to his door and asked him to go quickly to see a fellow in the village who was dying and asking for the preacher. The minister recognized the name. He hurried. The man, he remembered, had been a ruffian in his youth—a hooligan!

The minister stood by the man's bed. "Thank you for coming, Pastor." The voice was weak. "I asked for you to come because I need your forgiveness." There was a pause. "I need your forgiveness because 25 years ago on a stormy November night, I knocked on your door and sent you on a dangerous and unnecessary errand."

The minister replied, "That was long ago, and it has been long forgotten." He added, "But I do forgive you," and spoke to the man about the forgiveness that is offered by Jesus.

The man's breath came in short gasps. "But, tell me, Pastor, who were the other two who went with you that dark night?"

"There were no others," replied the minister. "I went alone."

Again there was a restless and labored pause. Then the man said, "No, we watched you—I and all five of my friends who were in

Late one stormy November night there came an urgent knocking.

on the hoax. We definitely saw you walking between two others. We saw them clearly. I have often wondered who they were."

Again there was a pause. The minister, skilled by experience in being a good listener, waited. After a moment the dying man opened his eyes for the last time. He could not speak above a whisper. He said, "They were dressed in white."

For he will command his angels concerning you to guard you in all your ways; they will lift you up in their hands, so that you will not strike your foot against a stone (Ps. 91:11-12).

28 | The State of Matrimony

The first car I ever (half) owned was a 15-year-old, 1921 Model-T Ford. A friend and I each plunked down two dollars and fifty cents, and the thing was ours to share. On alternate weeks it was all mine. My pastor looked at it and smiled. "I'd like to give it a name," I said. He suggested "Theodocia." He winked at my father, smiled, and said, "It means 'gift of God.'"

My gift of God was always breaking down or having flat tires or both. I drove my very first date to a symphony concert in it. Afterward, it refused to move. I found a rusted and disconnected battery cable under the wooden floor by the backseat. My date volunteered to help. She climbed into the back, and, with a stick I had found, she held the cable in place while I, lonely in the front, drove her home. Without her help, we would never have gone anywhere at all.

A few years later—50 years ago this month, to be exact (Nov. 10, 1940)—the two of us drove, minus Theodocia, into the state of matrimony. It is the oldest and largest of states, even though almost half of those entering it nowadays move out again. Contemplating our golden wedding anniversary, I find myself marveling about marriage. What a change the state of matrimony brings! For a long time you're not married, and then, suddenly, you're married all the time!

A recent headline in the newspaper said that the city of brotherly love—Philadelphia—is almost bankrupt. There are those who maintain that the state of marriage is in the same sad condition. They say that it ought to be abolished, or, at least, that its laws should be amended. There are those citizens of the matrimonial state who are bored, who maintain that monogamy is monotony.

Then there are those who don't like the weather there. They say that the state of matrimony has fewer sunny days than does the state of Michigan. The atmosphere is heavy, the skies brood with thunder and lighting, and the barometer is always falling. The (honey)moon over the state of matrimony—high and full at first— fades and sets, as is the habit of moons.

> There is nothing so annoying as when your spouse goes right on talking when you are interrupting.

Those who live in the state's valleys rather than on its mountaintops never see the moon again. Too bad!

The constitution of the matrimonial state grants all of its citizens opportunities to pursue happiness, but not all of them capture it. These are the ones who were married not by the state's justice of the peace but by its secretary of war.

But if the state of matrimony brings out the worst in its citizens, it can also bring out the best. Of course, life in that state is sometimes a hard pull. Yet we face few worthwhile goals that have no obstacles. It is true that there is nothing so annoying as when your spouse goes right on talking when you are interrupting. And married people must practice tolerance because, after all, spouses are entitled to their ridiculous opinions.

When all is said and done, success in this, the largest and oldest of states, consists not only in finding but also in being the right mate. Those who are successful will always keep working on their relationships. Those who rest on their laurels are wearing them in the wrong place.

The pitfalls in the state of marriage are many. Money is just one of them. Two can live as cheaply as one—but only for half as long.

Erma Bombeck marveled about a couple who had lived successfully in the matrimonial state for 50 years. How did they love each other all that time—through fevers, fatness, nausea, and irritability? Didn't they argue for 50 years about who would sleep next to the wall in the bedroom? Didn't they ever get tired of each other's jokes and hearing about each other's aches and pains?

A little girl touched on a good rule for marriage. "What is your father's name?" asked the teacher. "Daddy," she replied. "I know that," said the teacher, "but what does your mother call him?" The little girl's reply is worth remembering: "Mother doesn't call him anything. She likes him."

The apostle Paul wrote something very helpful for those who live in the state of matrimony. He defined love not so much as a feeling but as something that is done regardless of feeling. He said that love is an act of the will that reveals itself in things like patience, kindness, and good manners. Understood in such terms, a wedding is an act, but a marriage is an achievement.

These are some of my thoughts as I contemplate the golden wedding anniversaries of those whose beauty may have faded from their faces but not their hearts. As for our own 50th, for half a century my bride has been holding the cable to the battery. Without this, we would never have gone anywhere at all. Her name is not "Theodocia." But I do call her "Gift of God."

29 | A Missed Opportunity

D oodling is aimless scribbling. Some people do it with lines. I do it with words on my ever-present scratch pads. Ideas for sermons. Or for this column. Some notations are brief. Others grow like Topsy. Most end up in file 13. Some seem inspired when I write them, but a week later—not worth the paper they were written on. Altogether they keep my pen from getting rusty.

Recently we explored southern Indiana on a four-day jaunt. What a beautiful part of Hoosier land! Late one night I wrote some notes in a motel. What should I do with them? The wastebasket? *The Banner*? I'll try *The Banner*.

❧

11-1-01. We had a wonderful fish dinner today in a place on the banks of the mighty Ohio River. On the opposite shore stood the tall city of Louisville, Ky., with its stern-wheelers tethered and a sailboat in the foreground, tacking in the wind. They say that staring at water is therapeutic. I agree. We found it very restful to watch the restless current hurrying on its way downriver.

❧

With great animation, three men at an adjoining table were discussing the 2001 World Series. After the first two games, the New York Yankees were down 0-2. Now they are up 3-2 over the Arizona Diamondbacks and with only one more game to win to be, once again, crowned as world champions.

❧

Being an avid baseball fan, I couldn't help but eavesdrop. I had all I could do to refrain from inserting myself into their conversation when one of the men referred to a favorite player of mine as a "nincompoop." As I continued to listen, I found myself focusing more on their use of the King's English, whose rules for grammar were being clobbered, yet not without a degree of eloquence. "What say youse guys—the Yanks?" General agreement. Said one, "In de cards." Said the other, "Ah ain't got no use fer Colorado snakes."

⟡⟡

The waitress approached. She appeared to be Native American. After the coffee was served, I took a chance. I asked her if she had ever heard of Tecumseh. She said, "He was a great leader."

"Yes," I said. "He was a noble warrior. He was never a chief, but he was the bravest of the brave." The waitress took our orders and our menus and lingered.

"You know about him?" she asked.

I responded. "As a youth Tecumseh got hooked on firewater, but when he saw how useless it made him, he vowed never to touch the stuff again. And he never did."

The noise from the other table intruded. They couldn't agree on which pitcher was the best. The loudest voice said, "Ain't none of 'em no Sandy Koufax."

Meanwhile, the waitress had hunkered down so that we were at eye level. "Tell me more," she said.

"Many captured whites were burned at the stake. Tecumseh put a stop to it. One time when some braves were about to do it anyway, Tecumseh kicked the flaming brush away. The white man, tied and terrified, took hope. But Tecumseh was challenged. Bent on their evil deed, there were too many for him to control. Tecumseh wheeled and shot the prisoner dead through the head, thus sparing the poor man

> I had planned to lead the conversation from premonition to providence to the gospel.

untold agony and thwarting unholy desires. They never crossed Tecumseh again."

At the other table the three wise men were taking some other braves—the Atlanta Braves—apart. They couldn't survive the playoffs. Said one, "Not in de cards."

I called the attention of the waitress to the land of Kentucky across the Spaylaywitheepi (the Shawnee name for the Ohio River)—the land of Daniel Boone. Pointing to it, I said that Tecumseh wanted the white man to stay on that side of the river and leave this side to the "Indians." A treaty was drawn up to that effect, but the white man broke the treaty.

There was a young white who started farming on this side of the Spaylaywitheepi. One day, in danger of being scalped, he ran ahead of his pursuers till he came to a cliff. Standing there at hesitation point, he chose death by jumping rather than scalping. But he landed in the resilient branches of a tree, unharmed. He survived to tell about it and lived to the ripe old age of 48.

"Really?"

"Yes," I said. "Really."

"But what about Tecumseh?"

I told her more, including something about his no-good one-eyed brother and about Tecumseh's failure to unite the tribes against encroaching white men and his premonition the night before he died in battle somewhere in the vicinity of Chatham, Ontario, in the War of 1812. The night before that battle he sensed that he would die. And he did.

She left. When she returned with the bill she was pressed—very busy. I had planned to lead the conversation from premonition to providence to the gospel. But there was no more opportunity.

When we left, I caught her wondering glance: "How does that man know so much about Tecumseh?" I had not told her that I had just finished reading about his life (*A Sorrow in Our Heart: The Life of Tecumseh* by Allan Eckert; Bantam, 1992).

I had told her much about Tecumseh. And nothing about Jesus.

A missed opportunity.

30 | Ever Seeking, Never Finding

My scissors broke! They had cut my nails for 40 years, but last week they quit! Laid down on the job! Halfway through the nail on my pinkie, they just fell apart. A small tragedy!

I was fond of my scissors. I set out to replace them. The clerk in the store showed me all kinds of scissors and nail clippers, but I wanted a duplicate of what I had. Viewing my broken scissors with cold eyes, the clerk said that they were old-fashioned and out-of-date. "They don't make 'em like that no more," she said. She was chewing gum.

I was told the same news in the next store. And the next. But then I found a clerk who was more sympathetic. "I know a place where you might find one just like it," he said. He mentioned a store that was about 5 miles east of town.

"Yup," said the salesman 5 miles east of town. "I think you might find one at our warehouse. They've got a collection of old models."

"Where is the warehouse?" I asked. He gave me the address. It was about 10 miles west of town.

Ten miles west of town, the man at the warehouse said I was lucky because he was just about to close up. I showed him my broken scissors. He recognized them. He said they had stopped making straight blades. Curved blades were in now. "Tell you what," he said, "let me send your scissors to our supplier in New Jersey to be fixed. It'll take about a month."

I hesitated. I thought I might never see my scissors again. "I've got another idea," the man said. "Try a place where they fix watches. They might be able to help you."

Eureka! Why hadn't I thought of that? I knew of a jewelry store downtown where they repaired watches. Into the car again. East. West. Now downtown.

All those miles for nothing. All that time I had been on a wild goose chase!

The watch repairman in the jewelry store studied me through his magnifying glass, which seemed permanently attached to his head. Next he studied my broken scissors. "Can't help you," he said.

I drove home. All those miles for nothing. All that time I had been on a wild goose chase!

Remembering my promise to bring home some milk, I stopped at the local mall, which is within walking distance of our house. On an impulse, I walked into the optometrist's place first and showed my broken scissors. The clerk, who had fixed a hinge on my glasses the week before, took a look, took the scissors, disappeared, then reappeared. "All fixed," she said. "No charge."

I felt sheepish. Later that evening, while cutting my fingernails with my 40-year-old scissors, I thought of someone who had left not only our church, but the faith. Since then he's been everywhere looking for the truth, trying all kinds of religions, going East and West—ever seeking, never finding—while all the time what he is seeking is right here, back home, in the church he left.

And there's no charge.

31 | The Milk (Pea Soup) of Human Kindness

It was Tuesday. My wife's birthday. We were going out for dinner. Could I take her out for lunch too? She said she would like some pea soup. Bingo! I had certificates from a splendid emporium, way across town. Pea soup was on their menu for the day. I really think my wife said pea soup because she knows I like it. Nice wife.

We set out for the other side of town. The weather was inhospitable. The traffic was worse, and the place was hard to find. My wife tells me I'm too impatient. The fact is that we could have found gallons of pea soup on our side of town. When we finally got to where we were going, I discovered that the menu had changed. No pea soup on Tuesdays anymore. Nor would the certificates work. They were for goods in the rest of the store and not acceptable in the deli section. It was turning out to be one of those days!

My wife ordered chicken soup. How prosaic can you get? After struggling to find where we were headed and having fought traffic and bad weather, I wasn't going to settle for plain old chicken soup. Instead I ordered an exotic south-of-the-border potion that scorched my mouth and made my teeth look like rows of burned briquettes.

A nice lady approached our table. Was I me? The one who wrote in *The Banner*? I pled guilty. With a mouth on fire I tried not to blow flames in her direction. She said some nice things and disappeared.

Soon she returned with another lady in tow. A dark-haired lady. This time I remembered my manners and stood up. They talked "Cabbages." I talked bad weather, worse traffic, a hard-to-find place, certificates that didn't work, and torched tonsils. The ladies were most solicitous. But most people don't like to hear about other people's troubles.

Later that day dinner made up for the debacle at noon.

The next morning I was looking out the window and reviewing the day before. Who was that in the driveway, approaching our door? I recognized her. It was the dark-haired lady with whom I had shared my tale of woe. And what was she carrying?

> Who was that in the driveway? And what was she carrying?

I opened the door. The dark-haired one had made a pot of pea soup for us. She had traveled miles from a suburb across town just to bring an offering of pea soup! It was the day before Thanksgiving, and she had much to do.

Suddenly she was gone. In the brief conversational exchange she had mentioned her church. I called the pastor and explained. He knew who it might be. I sent a thank-you note.

What a nice thing for her to do! Every day we read of atrocities, murders, rapes, and robberies. Man's inhumanity to man, including that brew in the Bible served to a brother by one whose name I bear and filled with the milk of unkindness (Gen. 25:29-34).

What seldom gets reported is man's humanity to man—the many kindnesses shown in any community during the course of any day. Wayside ministries. Countless courtesies. Thoughtful gestures. Over the years we've had others at our doors with assorted soups and stuff.

The next time I sing "Auld Lang Syne" and come to the words "We'll tak' a cup o' kindness yet," I'll think of that dark-haired lady at the door with her elixir of green gold. A cup o' kindness! Pea soup!

An Eppinga family favorite

32 | Mezuzah

It was time to give the Father's Day sermon. I had also been asked to present a children's message to fit the day. For a preacher, preparing the latter can be as challenging and formidable as preparing the former. A word to the little ones should not exceed the length of their attention spans—two to three minutes. Alas, about the same attention span of some adults! But those two to three minutes had better be good, for a word to the children is often appraised as critically by some adults as the sermon that follows. Indeed, what is aimed at the children often registers better and longer with their elders!

This time I had no worries about the forthcoming children's message. I would simply show the little ones my mezuzah. It is a small object that can be hung on a doorframe. It can be opened to reveal a small scroll containing the words of Deuteronomy 6:4-9 in Hebrew. This passage addresses mainly parents, telling them to teach God's laws to their children around the clock—when they are standing, sitting, or lying down—and to place them on the doorframes of their houses.

It was my plan to open my mezuzah, show the children the scroll, and tell them that many Jewish parents still place their mezuzahs on the front doors of their houses. Going out and coming in, they touch them in order to remind themselves of what the Lord commands. Then I would tell the children to be thankful for Christian fathers who, although they have no mezuzahs hanging on their doorframes, nevertheless do what God requires. It would be a good Father's Day message for the children.

On Saturday night I took my trusty mezuzah out of my desk drawer so that I wouldn't forget it the next morning. But, ready for church the following day, I couldn't find it. My wife insisted that she had not touched it. "But it just can't walk away by itself!" I said. I was in a panic! I couldn't leave without my mezuzah! My children's message would be a flop! I searched desperately until the clock demanded that I leave. Preachers can't be late for services. Reluctantly and profoundly depressed, I slid into my car. Dumb! Dumb! Dumb! How could I lose what I had laid ready the night before?

> I am presently in the market for a new mezuzah.

The service began. The children's moment arrived. I came down to meet the little ones. Without my mezuzah, I did the next best thing. I described it. I walked over to the nearest doorframe and pretended to touch it. Young, uncomprehending eyes followed me. The children went back to their pews. I went back to the pulpit. Dumb! Dumb! Dumb!

Returning home, I renewed my search. Some family members arrived for dinner and joined in. We removed the pillows from the davenport. Under? Maybe. Nope. No mezuzah. Ending the search, we clung to the faint hope that it might yet show up. Somewhere. Sometime.

Monday I drowned my sorrows on the golf course. When I arrived home, my wife met me at the door with the announcement that the lost had been found. In the washing machine! My mezuzah had been with me the whole Sunday. In my shirt pocket! Dumb! Dumb! Dumb!

Alas, the scroll was soaking wet. I put it in the oven to dry. I should have consulted those scientists who so carefully restored the Dead Sea Scrolls. My scroll came out of the oven dry and brittle. If I had tried to unroll it, it would have shattered in pieces.

I thought that moist air might make it supple again. I thought of my father's humidor, which prevented his cigars from drying out. Would a humidor do the trick?

When the scroll had been sufficiently moistened, I unrolled it ever so gently, proud of my ingenuity. But, horrors, the scroll was empty! Deuteronomy 6:4-9 was gone! Our Maytag had erased the Word of the Lord!

I am presently in the market for a new mezuzah. Meanwhile, I am grateful that neither Maytag nor anything else can expunge the Word. Contrary to many opinions of the day, the Bible is not written in disappearing ink. Jesus said, "I tell you the truth, until heaven and earth disappear, not the smallest letter, not the least stroke of a pen, will by any means disappear from the Law until everything is accomplished" (Matt. 5:18).

33 | Excommunication

It was a decade ago. I found myself in a place in Florida that held an overabundance of Christian Reformed snowbirds. I well remember that first morning when I took a walk on the beach—or tried to. Every 10 or 20 steps I bumped into yet another Christian Reformer who wished to engage me in a discussion on the state of the church. The same thing happened back home in malls, churches, golf clubs, restaurants—everywhere. It was a time of denominational upheaval with the women-in-office issue on everyone's lips.

Today we don't talk much about the state of the church or even denominational issues, though there are many pressing ones. Too bad. But last week it happened again. A stranger, recognizing me, wanted to pick my brain on the subject of church discipline. Someone in his church had been excommunicated. He was irate. "We don't do that anymore. It's old-fashioned," he said. He remembered how, years ago, a young couple had been made to stand before the minister and publicly confess to breaking the seventh commandment. He said he was glad that we had graduated from such heavy-handed ways. "But now," he added, "it looks like we're back in the excommunication business again."

There was much in what he said with which I could agree. Too often in the past, church discipline was practiced in authoritarian ways. The zeal to maintain the purity of the church is commendable. Discipline is, after all, one of the marks of a true church.

But the spirit in which church discipline was practiced often lacked love. And one of the purposes of excommunication—namely, the salvation of the sinner (1 Cor. 5:5)—was often lost sight of. As

129

one subject of church discipline told me years ago, "I was booted out, after which I was shunned like a leper." I was sorry that the members of his church did not understand that what was done was presumably motivated by a Christian concern, as stated in the formulary for excommunication: "Count him not as an enemy but at times admonish him as you would a brother."

Alas, all of this has seldom been understood and practiced. And so the church fathers, in an effort to improve matters, deleted the word *excommunications* from the statistical section of the Christian Reformed Church *Yearbook.* Excommunications, of which there are few, are now included in the category of *reversions*—those former members who no longer attend any church at all.

My objection fell on deaf ears. Getting rid of *excommunication,* I said, would weaken the practice of church discipline. I was told that *reversion* was a euphemism for *excommunication.* But the words in question are not synonymous. A reversion is a changing back to former ways. It is an act on the part of the person reverting. Excommunication, on the other hand, is an act of the church—a prayerful act of exclusion as a hopeful means toward eventual inclusion.

I learned all of this intellectually in seminary. But I learned it better years ago from a young lady who saved her marriage. I was her pastor. One day she called me, as she had done many times before, to discuss her marital situation. She loved her husband, a man I deemed unworthy of her affections. I couldn't see why she loved him. My private opinion was that he was a dolt. I had met with them together a number of times in an effort to save the marriage. But each time,

> **"Pastor, the only way to get him back is to put him out."**

after promising to make amends, the dolt would "revert"—going back to the bottle and other women.

She called me to tell me what she had done. She had secretly removed the house key from his key ring. He had gone out for the evening but didn't know that he wasn't getting back in. I tried halfheartedly to dissuade her, but she was adamant. I have never forgotten her response: "Pastor, the only way to get him back is to put him out."

Early the next morning, around two o'clock, her husband called me to tell me that he had been locked out. I invited him over. We talked and drank coffee. Afterward, I put him up for what was left of the night. Doing so, I asked him how it was that he had called me. He said he wouldn't have done so except for the fact that his wife had posted a note on the locked door. It said, "Call Rev. Eppinga."

True excommunication is like that. The Lord, through his church to which he has entrusted the keys of the kingdom, sometimes needs to lock somebody out. But when he does, he always posts a note on the locked door. It says,

"Call my Son."

34 | Verne Barry

When I became pastor of a large downtown church, I soon became aware of the existence of the "street people," as they were called. I remember looking out my study window that first day and seeing two bedraggled-looking men sharing a bottle in an alley.

On Sundays I faced a well-dressed congregation. But during the week people from another world came knocking on the church door.

I made a feeble effort in those early days to bridge the gap between "us" and "them." Every Thursday afternoon I sat on a downtown bench for a few hours. I was surprised at how many people stopped to chat.

I met Jim Hall, who, with his charms, could have owned the town if not for a mental disorder. He came to our church and stayed until he died. He always had candy for the children and always appeared at church dinners with his windup record player and scratchy Bing Crosby records.

There was Levi Perry, who also adopted us. He had the mind of a child but knew enough to say on Good Fridays, "This is the day He died." We taught him to add, "For me."

There was 5-foot Hezekiah—that's what they called him—who wore a big hat and a coat so large it dragged behind him. He too became a faithful attender. People seated behind him saw nothing but the hat.

I also remember John Jellema, a church member who visited drunks in cheap hotels, sometimes with me in tow.

In much later years there was Abe De Vries, also a member of our church, who exercised a "doorstep" ministry. With funds from the deacons, he provided aid to people from the neighborhood who came to our doors. Other members, too, were active in reaching out to needs so great that we might as well have tried emptying the Pacific Ocean with a spoon.

> As a Manhattan executive, he had it all. Then he lost it.

Enter Verne Barry. As a Manhattan executive, he had it all. He operated a flock of limos in New York City. He transported the likes of Frank Sinatra, Dean Martin, Liz Taylor, Lucille Ball, Elvis Presley, Bob Hope, members of the British royal family, and other heads of state.

Though he sat on top of the world, his one-martini lunches gradually turned to two-, three-, and four-, plus cocktails at countless black-tie affairs. The end was inevitable. He lost it all. Including his family.

Verne found himself on the streets, sleeping in homeless shelters and standing in line at soup kitchens. Eventually he landed in our town, near to family members, yet found no life of sobriety. He slept in a cardboard box beneath a bridge. Occasionally—so he told me—he appeared at our church doors after services, seeking a handout.

Then Providence stepped in. Through contact with Christians and with God's help, his life turned around. He found a new aim, which was to help the homeless and drifters. He founded Faith Inc., a nonprofit agency to help the homeless earn paychecks and dignity.

Verne wrote his life story in the hope of inspiring others to give a hand up instead of a handout to people whom Jesus called "the least of these." It appeared under the title *Faith: Reflections on Being Down but Never Out* (PublishAmerica, Baltimore).

He became a force in the community. The mayor appointed him a member of the Downtown Development Authority and, later, its chair. I watched him take men off the street in his storefront office and put them to work. Sundays he sat in our church. A member. But then came physical problems. A wheelchair. Diabetes. Amputations.

He eagerly looked forward to the appearance of his book. But when it did finally see the light of day, he was too sick to hold it in his hand. Then he died.

The story of Verne Barry would be enough make me a Christian if I weren't one already. God can make new men and new women. He gives us new hearts, as only he can.

How I wish the Lord had not taken Verne at age 70. Still, God knows best. And he can raise up others like Verne.

Meanwhile, as Verne always said:

"Let people who live in the sun always pay attention to those who live in the shadows."

A $19 million studio-apartment complex for individuals with special needs was completed in 2007 and named the Verne Barry Place. It is located in downtown Grand Rapids, Michigan, on the same street where, as a homeless drunk, Verne wandered during the day and slept at night.

35 | The Barrel

During World War II days, the Andrews Sisters made the Hit Parade with their song "Roll Out the Barrel" (... *we'll have a barrel of fun*). But although their song made the top-10, it never made the *Psalter Hymnal*. This despite the fact that, on occasion, many Christian Reformed ministers rolled out their barrels. Let me explain.

By way of a circuitous route, I was finally declared eligible for a call in our denomination. I soon received two calls, one from a large church of 212 families and another from a small church of 19 families. I felt immediately that the bigger church would be too much for a fledgling like me to handle. I had the energy but not the experience.

It was a day when many Christian Reformed ministers were workhorses. Some preached two or three sermons a week, taught most of the catechism classes, led the Men's Society, the Ladies' Aid, and did all or most of the annual home visits.

I consulted one such miracle worker, who, on top of everything else, typed up the worship bulletins and cranked them out on his old mimeograph machine late Saturday evenings. I asked him how he managed when, in the same week, he might have a wedding to perform and a funeral to conduct. He answered, "I roll out the barrel."

Definition: "A barrel in a parsonage is a repository for old sermons." I didn't have one. I took the 19 families.

I remember a seminary professor of that day who maintained that a minister's second charge was always a critical one. Having arrived with a full barrel, there was always the temptation of coasting—

preaching old homilies, thereby losing the momentum and creativity demanded when the barrel was bare.

The late Peter Eldersveld, our radio minister of a former day, speaking at a ministers' conference I attended, noted that some members of the venerable clergy, forced by circumstance to fish one out of the barrel, would choose a poor one, hoping it was forgotten. "Wrong," said Eldersveld. "So what if they are remembered? Good messages bear repetition." The late novelist Peter De Vries, listening to the old ones, remarked that they had great sedative powers. He added, "Many new ones too."

When my 19 families moved to a new location, constructing their own building, I was busier than a one-armed paperhanger. I leaned on my barrel more than once. I told my wife that if the house caught fire, I'd rescue my barrel first. After that, women and children. But old sermons require resuscitation, reworking, revival—making even more work than preparing a new one.

Today I look into my full barrel and think of the hours and hours its contents represent. A big part of my life lies in that barrel. How did I write so many sermons? One answer is to say, "One page at a time." Some would slide out of my typewriter with relative ease. More often they were slow going. And still are. Sometimes it takes considerable time just to find the right word.

I wonder how many people listened to all those words. How many of those words went in one ear and out the other? Was it all worth it?

When I harbor such thoughts, I'm always comforted by the following story.

> I told my wife that if the house caught fire, I'd rescue my barrel first.

A minister confided to a friend. He said he'd been preaching for 60 years. What good did it all do? What a lot of work went into all that preaching! He couldn't even remember most of his own sermons, so how could he expect they were worth all that time and effort?

His friend responded, "I've eaten my wife's cooking for 60 years. I can't remember most of the meals, but they nourished me day after day and week after week."

What a wonderful story for all preachers. And for preachers to come—a challenging thought.

36 | Things

The world is so full of a number of things, I think we should all be as happy as kings.

—Robert Louis Stevenson

I have an attachment to things. I have a shrunken, petrified piece of an eraser I bought in high school. I wouldn't part with it for anything. Next to it, in my desk drawer, is a small paper airplane my mother bought for me when I was small. I possess many other things as well, both old and new. Some I use. Some I just look at. But whether useful or just decorative, I couldn't do without things. I am not pure spirit floating in air, with no need for coats, books, beds, toothbrushes, and more. I need things. We all do.

I'm not a pack rat. I knew a parishioner who saved all his newspapers. There was no room in his house to sit down and visit. We stood outside. I'm not like that. I'm not even a saver like some people I know, who collect stamps or old coins or baseball cards.

If my wife and I moved into a smaller place, as we sometimes think we should, what would happen to all our things? People have estate sales. They get rid of all their things. How do they do it? It seems heartless. What would happen to my books? What would happen to my blue marbles that I hold in my hand to play with whenever I am trying to dream up another "Cabbage" for *The Banner*—like this one?

Not only do I have things. I personify them. They take on a life of their own. I talk to my car and pat it on its hood whenever it has safely transported me from point A to point B. I'm sad to think of some of my old cars sitting forlornly in junkyards. I pat my books.

141

The first book I ever wrote was titled *The Soul of the City*. It wasn't much—mostly blank pages. But it sold well. I met up with a copy of it recently. I was visiting a secondhand bookstore in Chicago. In front, by the sidewalk, stood a large bin filled with books for 5 cents each. I fished in it. Off the bottom, I came up with—surprise!—a copy of *Soul of the City*. It looked quite

> I have a shrunken, petrified piece of an eraser I bought in high school.

the worse for wear. I went in and redeemed my own book for a nickel. Today it sits on one of my shelves, grateful to be home. But I wonder, Who bought it? How many people owned it? Did anyone read it? And who dumped it so unceremoniously into the bottom of that bin? Books talk. But mine won't. It refuses to tell me what happened to it along the way. I wish I knew. Things, such as books, have histories. Just like people.

I remember the story of a check written long ago to a college student by a leading citizen of the town. The needy student had shoveled snow from the man's sidewalk. The check was made out for 10 cents! Hilarious. The student showed it to his friends. One of them bought it for a dollar—just to show it around. A prominent merchant, a rival of the check writer, bought it for $5 and displayed it in his store window. The writer of the check, embarrassed, bought it from his nasty rival for $25—just to get rid of it. Things, as I say, have histories.

What about things in the life of Christ? I believe that God, in his wisdom, destroyed them lest we worship them as sacred objects. Still, there is the story of Jesus' robe. There is the Shroud of Turin, in which the body of Jesus was supposedly wrapped. And there are enough pieces of the cross of Christ in churches, temples, and shrines here and there to build a whole block of houses. All bogus.

On the day I die, the Lord will separate me from all my earthly things. My piece of an eraser. My paper airplane. My house. My books. My car. Everything! I thank God for the use of them in the here and now; I could not get along very well without them. But when angels bear my soul to heaven, by God's grace, the heavenly chariot will not be pulling a U-Haul.

37 | Rookie

A rookie police officer has a little training but no experience. Same thing goes for a rookie preacher. A few weeks ago one of them—a beginner fresh out of seminary—asked me for some advice. His question brought me back to my own rookie days.

In my second year at Westminster Seminary in Philadelphia, I became the student preacher of Atonement Presbyterian Church. It was a small congregation of 40 people, plus or minus. They met weekly in a small all-purpose room on the second floor of a building in the downtown area of South Philly. It was not a very friendly environment. My duties also included being a rookie janitor, plus I played the piano whenever the regular pianist couldn't be present. My stipend was three dollars a week.

I came early on Sunday mornings to open all the windows and air out the place. Whatever group met on Saturday evenings left behind a stale odor of beer and cigarettes. I hauled a pulpit out of a closet, which also held the Bibles and hymnbooks to be used by the coming worshipers. After sweeping the floor, I lined up about 50 chairs in three rows and positioned the piano. After all this, I stood at the top of the stairs as a committee of one to welcome the worshipers.

Those who came submitted themselves patiently to my ministrations. You might say that for me it was an on-the-job learning experience. I soon developed a pattern of sermon preparation: Text selection. Text research. Writing out the sermon in full. Outlining the sermon. Adjusting the sermon, if necessary, to improve its logic as suggested by the outline. Memorizing the outline in order to leave the manuscript at home.

I tried honing my outline into three points, which was the style of Christian Reformed preaching in those days. I also practiced preaching my masterpiece to the foot-high statue of a boy, complete with baseball cap slightly askew, that stood on my

> She felt that my pulpit appearance left something to be desired.

desk—a reminder to keep it simple. Another reminder was the word *Christocentric* jotted down somewhere in the margin to ensure the message I made would be Christ-centered.

After rolling the old pulpit back into the closet and setting all things aright in what I called "the upper room," I headed for the subway. This meant passing the house of a church member, obviously encased in a corset, who was preoccupied with my physical condition. She had dedicated herself to—as she put it—"putting some fat on that young man." She felt that my pulpit appearance left something to be desired.

In those days there was a nationally known musician named Fred Waring. Fred and his excellent singers were known as "Fred Waring and His Pennsylvanians." Mr. Waring turned out to be a man of many talents. Fred had invented a food blender known as the Waring blender. It became a national hit. Many people bragged about their Waring blender, including the lady with the corset whose calling it was to fatten me up.

I had promised that on my way to the subway I would stop in at her place so she could hit me with her blender. Today my taste buds still remember her concoction—a blend of carrots and spinach, which she called her "cocktail" for me. Alas, her objective was not achieved. I stayed at 130 pounds.

Today I look back at that small band of worshipers with delight. A happy memory. Their previous pastor had questioned the historicity of the resurrection. They were astute enough to recognize a heresy and did something about it.

I count them as heroes in my past.

38 | Sunday School

Have you ever been personally confronted with the gospel? Asked whether you have invited Jesus into your heart? Asked whether you love him and have given yourself to him?

That happened to me a long time ago. To tell you about it, I have to reach way back to Robert Raines. He lived in Gloucester, England. He is regarded as the father of modern Sunday school.

In a time of child labor, many children were released from their grinding work on the Sabbath. Some of them, loitering on filthy streets, presented an abject sight to Raines. With the aid of a few local women, he gathered some of these children into his house for some Christian instruction.

He held his first class in 1781. Only five years later some 250,000 children throughout the land attended these Sunday schools.

God blessed Raines's missionary outreach, and it spread to other lands. In the United States, the American Sunday School Union was formed. By the beginning of the past century, 11 million children were enrolled in Sunday schools.

In the Netherlands, the Sunday school (Zondag school) also appeared and flourished. But leaders of the Reformed churches made a sharp distinction. Sunday school was a missionary effort aimed at children who came from unchurched families. Catechism classes, on the other hand, were for covenant children. The latter were therefore not enrolled, nor sent, to Sunday school. Covenant children were not missionary objects. To treat them as such would be to ignore or deny the covenant. Consequently my father, growing up in the Netherlands, went to catechism, not Sunday school.

When my father came to America and to the Christian Reformed Church, and when he became the father of me, this distinction remained sharp in his mind. Therefore, when all the children in our church attended both Sunday school and catechism classes, I attended only the latter. After morning services, while my friends had to stay for Sunday school, I gleefully went home with my parents.

Getting a little older, I began to reassess my advantage over my friends. They seemed to be having fun. They received Sunday school pins at the end of the season and wore them proudly. I had none. They had picnics. Catechism classes didn't. Clearly I was missing out. I asked my father for permission to go to Sunday school, and permission was granted. I have an idea that he felt wisdom dictated a compromise.

Sunday school was a new experience for me. First we all met together in a session led by the Sunday school superintendent. We sang. He spoke. He rang a bell. That was the signal for all to head for their own classrooms spread throughout the building. I followed Harold, my friend, and soon found myself in a small cubbyhole with some other boys. Then the teacher appeared. Bert!

Bert was a carpenter. A good one. He worked for my father. A nice man and devout. I remembered overhearing him once when he said to my father, "When my wife and I can't sleep, we sit up in bed and sing a psalm." I thought that was strange, but that was before I discovered the power of—and my love for—those psalms. I enjoyed Bert's teaching. Bible stories—more fun than catechism, where we sat in awe of the minister. And always there was an application.

> No one in all those years ever confronted me personally with the gospel.

One day after the bell rang and we were all dismissed, Bert took me aside. "Stay with me for just a minute," he said. I wondered what was up. We huddled. Then he talked to me about Jesus. He asked whether I loved him and if I had invited him into my heart. Then he prayed. He asked me to say a prayer. Later I found out that he did this with all his boys.

Bert wasn't aware of the distinction drawn by the Reformed churches in the Netherlands—that Sunday school was for the "heathen." In those few minutes Bert treated me, a covenant child, as a mission object. Today, in retrospect, I'm glad he did. The church of my early years was a great blessing in my life. But no one in all those years ever confronted me personally with the gospel. No preacher. No elder.

Only Bert.

How many people in how many churches are never brought face to face with Jesus?

∽⟲⟳∼

Have you ever been personally confronted with the gospel? Asked whether you have invited Jesus into your heart? Asked whether you love him and have given yourself to him?

I ask you now.

39 | Heaven

I don't much care for those pearly-gate stories people tell. But there are exceptions. Like Hank's dream. Hank dreamed that he died and went to heaven. They had a lot of organs up there. God invited Hank to play the biggest and the best. That was right down Hank's alley. He had been a church organist on earth for 60 years.

Seated on that heavenly organ bench, Hank felt the old skills flowing back into his fingers. His creaking knees grew supple again as his feet glided over the pedals. He played a psalm and, suddenly, angels came and sang as he played. Then old Hank woke up and the dream was gone. When he told others his dream, he said that he truly believed that every day he was one day closer to its realization. A reporter heard him say that and put it in the paper (*Centraal Weekblad*, January 1997).

I like what Hank said. But is that what heaven will be like? Are there organs there? I remember a catechumen who asked me if people played golf up there and if all their drives went straight. Being a duffer, I mused on that. I wouldn't mind breaking par once.

Isaiah and John present us with pictures of heaven. The poet Milton leaned on Ezekiel when he wrote about heaven. Despite these glimpses, Dante tells us about Pope Gregory I arriving in heaven and being amused to discover that his theory on the hierarchy of angels was all wrong. As it turned out, he knew very little about it. Me too. But—although I'm no pope—I know for certain about three surprises that await me in heaven.

The first two will be the discovery of the absence of some I was certain would be there, and the presence of some I was sure would not be there. The third surprise will be that I am there.

> I know for certain about three surprises that await me in heaven.

Maybe old Hank isn't so far off the mark. Jesus talked about heaven a lot. Not surprisingly, for it was his home. He would often say, "The kingdom of heaven is like . . ." and then compare it to some earthly thing. Look around. Earth is in the image of heaven, just as we are in the image of God. Anglican Harry Blamires said, "Earthly life is littered with glimpses of heaven." And poet Elizabeth Browning wrote, "Earth's crammed with heaven and every common bush afire with God."

Makes sense! I've seen a house designed by Frank Lloyd Wright in Chicago and another in Grand Rapids, Michigan. They are very different, yet I can tell that the same architect created both. They have some things in common. Just so with earth and heaven. Same architect.

What's important, of course, is how to get to heaven. You can get there, as someone said, without health, wealth, fame, education, culture, beauty, friends, and ten thousand other things. But you cannot get there without Jesus. He is the only way.

Who knows? Maybe when we get there, we'll hear Hank play the organ.

40 | Of Death and Grace

I am dying. Of cancer. This past Christmas was my last. Spring always has been my favorite season. At this writing, I hope to see the spring of 2008. Since childhood, I have loved baseball. Today my marvelous palliative-care physician told me there is a chance that I will watch my dear Detroit Tigers on television on opening day. But that I will not see the World Series.

To paraphrase a great English observer of human nature, Samuel Johnson, the prospect of dying focuses one's thinking. What follows are some of my thoughts about death.

Primary among them is this: I don't want to die. Even though I have lived 90 years, two decades beyond the biblical three score and ten, I want to live. There are things yet that I want to do. People to see. Sermons to preach.

Also, I'm scared. Does it surprise you that a minister of the Christian Reformed Church is scared of dying? As a Christian, I do not fear death; still, I fear dying. How much will dying hurt? On a chart of 1 to 10, my pain threshold is a -100.

And I'm scared of something else—the money running out before life runs out.

Most of all, I'm scared about what will become of Anne, my beloved wife, who can't hear or walk or remember. For years I've asked God to let me outlive her, so I can take care of her until her home-going. Then, I have told him, I could go to my grave in peace.

But God has not answered my prayer in the fashion I have requested. My son says that God has, really, because so much of Anne already has been taken (although not her sweet disposition). I am not convinced by this line of reasoning and find but small comfort in it.

Those are the big things. There also are smaller things.

For example, I struggle with disappointment and embarrassment. Always having taken care of my family and myself, now others have to take care of me. My body is failing. My mind, too, is not as sharp as it used to be—particularly because of the medications for pain. (Still, even in this, I am forced to admit that I have reason for giving thanks. Our attentive children love their mother and father. And daughter Sue, upon ending her teaching career, has devoted herself to the care of her parents. And there is a special caregiver named Mary Ellen.)

Over my 63 years of ministry, I've been a pastor as well as a preacher. I've counseled parishioners, tried to comfort them, and conducted hundreds of funeral services. (I've always welcomed funeral services because, unlike at weddings, those in attendance actually listen to the Christian message, focused as they are for the moment upon their own mortality.) Now, however, it's my minister who counsels me, comforts me, and plans with me the details of my own funeral service.

And I ask myself, why do bad things happen to good people? Why me? Why now? There's so much for me yet to do.

Early in my ministry I attempted to answer that question, as it was posed to me by a grieving parent, a dying mother, a devastated family, a stunned congregation. But soon I came to recognize that my answers were unconvincing and maybe even misdirected.

Now I am older, I hope wiser, and facing my own death. I try to answer that question—Why do bad things happen to good people?—with three points. (Are you surprised?)

> As important as
> is the question
> about why God
> allows bad things
> to happen to
> good people,
> it is not the
> most important
> question in life.

First is a simple admission: I do not know. "There you have it, plain and flat," as poet John Greenleaf Whittier once wrote.

Second is a story that gives me just a tiny glimpse into an answer. I will be edified if it does the same for you. Here it is:

When I was a boy, I feared going to the dentist. My father took me there anyway. When I was sitting in the chair, my father near me, I begged my father to rescue me from what lay ahead. My father did not do so. Instead he told me that he loved me and that I would be all right. After that, all I could do was trust my father. My father knew what was above and beyond my understanding at the time—that I needed to go to the dentist.

In a similar fashion, tragedy and death are above and beyond my understanding. I pray for God to take them away. For some reason, God doesn't answer my prayers in the ways I want.

But here's the point. Above my understanding. But not God's. He loves me, this I know, so all I can do is trust him, my only comfort in life and death. My father knew, and my heavenly Father knows, things that were and are beyond my comprehension.

Third is my main point: As important as is the question about why God allows bad things to happen to good people, it is not the most important question in life. The most important question in life—in all the world and in all the universe, for that matter—is, rather, "Why does God allow a good thing to happen to bad people?"

I am a sinner—a bad person. Yet my Father gave his only Son for me—a very good thing indeed.

During a lifetime of ministry, I have heard the last words of many of my parishioners. One does not forget such things. The person whose last words I've been reflecting upon the most these past weeks is William Harry Jellema, a professor of philosophy at Calvin College and arguably the greatest mind in the history of the Christian Reformed Church. His last words—simple but not simplistic—were, "It's grace, Jake; it's all grace."

Think of it! The enormous intellect that was William Harry Jellema condensed the entire Bible, all of theology, and every last Reformed creed and confession into just one word: *grace.*

Thus the title of my last *Banner* article, my last "Of Cabbages and Kings" in a series stretching 40 years, is not "Of Death," but "Of Death and Grace." Of all the words I have shared with you over all the decades in these pages, dear readers, the ones I would leave with you are . . .

"May the grace of our Lord Jesus Christ, the love of God, and the fellowship of the Holy Spirit be with you all."

Amen.

Rev. Eppinga passed away March 1, 2008. The Detroit Tigers played their first game of the season March 31.

"The time has come," our Savior said,
"To show you many things:
The face of your Almighty God—
And Jesus Christ, your King—
And that the streets *are* paved with gold—
And angels *do* have wings."

—Deanna Eppinga DeVries
"For Dad: Welcome to Heaven," 2008